PROPERTY LADDER

Profit from Property

First published in Great Britain in 2003 by Cassell Illustrated, 2–4 Heron Quays, London E14 4JP
a division of Octopus Publishing Group Limited

A CIP catalogue record for this book is available from the British Library.

ISBN 1844031 918

Printed in Italy by Printer Trento S.r.l.

CONTENTS

Introduction

As the property bug appears to continue to sweep the nation, many of us are keen to find out how to turn property into profit.

Whether you are a first-time buyer, want to make the most of your own home or are serious about developing a property as a business venture, this is the book you need to guide you through the process.

Developing a property means changing it from one state into a more marketable one. It might sound simple, yet filming *Property Ladder* has shown us that, for many people, property development can be stressful, expensive, time-consuming and filled with unexpected problems. Drawn from my own personal experiences, real case studies from past and present series, as well as advice from estate agents and other professionals, this book is a user-friendly resource to guide you through the practicalities of developing property. It is full of no-nonsense advice, tips and practical 'how to' information to inspire and drive your project forward. And, because not every property has to be a money-making machine, there are also plenty of ideas for your own home.

Any aspiring property developer will be pleased to know that it is always *possible* to turn bricks and mortar into cash, in any market, anywhere in the world. But to do so you have to buy and sell at the right price and get all of your sums right in between. In the current market conditions, this has never been so important. If you are thinking of plunging your savings into property, always study the market before you dive in. Understanding how and why markets have changed in recent history is likely to stand you in very good stead for a lifetime of building ownership.

A brief history of the UK's property market

In the UK, over the last 100 years alone, diverse social, political and economic developments, as well as changes in demographics, have affected the property market dramatically.

It is possible to chart a 'Golden Age' that started in 1945 and ended in 1973 with the greatest national property boom of the century. At the end of World War II there was an initial recovery in all forms of production and an urgent need to build new housing, following the widespread destruction caused by bombing. Although the country faced economic hardship, this rise in production boosted employment levels and increased consumer spending.

In 1947, Clement Attlee's Labour government created pressure for the economy to grow by lowering interest rates. It simultaneously introduced a number of housing schemes such as building licensing, and encouraged the building of new homes, thereby influencing private sector investment. As such, the housing market had a significant impact on the uninterrupted growth of the period. Although the population had grown very little, building construction remained productive as many households divided after the war and an increasing number of family members sought separate accommodation. This economic climate continued almost uninterrupted until 1973 as interest rates drifted only very slowly upwards, inhibiting an economic relapse.

Home ownership had become a highly valued form of long-term investment, due to both the stability it offered following uncertain times and the economic climate of the day. With the onset of high inflation in the late 1960s, house prices took off at a dramatic rate. The pace levelled briefly in the mid 1970s before accelerating again. Far from the rise in the real value of houses acting as a brake on demand, the opposite occurred and an unprecedented scramble by the British public to own a home ensued.

conservative policy

When Margaret Thatcher took office as prime minister in 1979, inflation had begun to accelerate at an alarming rate. By the spring of 1980 it was well over 20%. Thatcher aimed to get Britain back on track, seeking economic recovery from the oil crisis and the 'winter of discontent' of 1973. The predominant aims of her policy were to master inflation and 'roll back the frontiers of the State', and the Conservatives sought to cut public expenditure, deregulate and privatise. The biggest reductions were seen in housing and social subsidies. Yet despite its efforts to curtail spending, the Government found itself obliged to spend heavily. Expenditure on social services and housing (excluding capital expenditure) increased from £36 billion in 1978–9 to £98 billion in 1987–8.

Thatcher pushed for 'housing for all'. Privatisation saw the sale of shares in the nationalised industries, which helped create a share-owning democracy, while the sale of council houses and the increased availability of mortgages helped to widen the class of property owners. Until the 1980s mortgages had been rationed and the market tightly controlled. Income multiples were strict – only one income was taken into account – and the lender made funds available only to those who had banked with the company for a period of time.

housing boom

After 1983 the British economy began to recover. Employment figures rose for seven successive years and consumer activity seemed to change. The public seemed to have more disposable income, were spending more and saving less. However, at the core of this fall in investment ratio was the national housing boom, which reached a peak in 1988. House prices rose to extraordinary levels – in the South of England at first and a little later in the North – in relation to average incomes. The growth in property prices and the prospect of its continuance enhanced the attractiveness of home ownership and added to its demand.

When inflation had accelerated in the 1970s house prices rose fivefold, faster even than earnings. By the early 1980s house prices were three and a half times earnings, rising to about four and a half times the figure for national incomes in 1988 (and more than five times earnings in London). The fact that house prices had increased by almost 75% between 1985 and 1988 was encouraging to borrowers, as long as they could rely on the value of their homes rising to set against their mortgage interest bills. However, in 1988 for the first time, the capital appreciation of the average home exceeded the average mortgage interest bill of £2,800 by £5,000. In other words, the real cost of borrowing was negative. In addition, the housing boom was being fuelled by easy access to borrowing. While building societies had offered mortgages to a wider sector of the public in the early 1980s, they now began to offer 100% mortgages. These mortgages alone grew from under £10 billion in 1980 to nearly £50 billion in 1988. But after 1988 the process went into reverse. High rates of interest on outstanding mortgages put pressure on consumer incomes while house prices either fell (particularly in the South-East) or stabilised (in the North).

During this period, the Government announced its plans to privatise pensions by the time the next generation of workers retired, claiming that the increasing population would make the current state system unsustainable. Having lost confidence in state pensions, a large sector of the population swiftly reinvested in stocks and shares. A sharp rise in the financial markets followed, despite any marked increase in manufacturing or industry. Shortly afterwards, the same markets started to fall under the stress of the false inflation, and a number of unscrupulous salesmen scandals, which cashed in on the public's desire to reinvest, were documented in the press. As the stock market crashed in October 1987, the public sought the answer to financial investment in the property market.

'buy to let' mortgages

Lenders responded to this increase in demand by creating specialist 'buy to let' mortgages. These packages offered preferential rates to individual investors who hoped to rent out their properties to build a pension for when they retired. Great swathes of the British public bought properties at the bottom end of the market, making it increasingly difficult for first-time buyers to get on the first rung of the property ladder. The demand for additional houses to 'buy to let' was the final boost to market prices as demand outstripped supply.

GROWTH IN HOME OWNERSHIP

During the period 1980–90 the traditional perception of who could own their own home changed dramatically. In 1981 home ownership among professional people, employers and managers was already at more than 80%. By 1995–6 the percentage of home ownership among junior non-manual workers had risen from 62 to 75% and among semi-skilled manual workers it had increased from 35 to 55%.

The late 1980s were years of prosperity in the British housing market. Consumers had disposable incomes, interest rates had been brought down to nominal terms after the stock market crash of October 1987, unemployment was low and mortgages were cheap. Furthermore, there were more properties on the market thanks to the selling off of social housing and a general increase in housing stock since the War. But the house prices-to-earnings ratio reached a peak at around five and a half (compared with the traditional rate of three to three and a half) and became unsustainable.

slump and revival

The collapse in house prices began in 1989 and the property market had just about run out of steam by 1993. A major contributory factor was the doubling of the nominal interest rate from 7.5 to 15%, which dramatically increased mortgage payments. The collapse of the housing market was dramatic. At the end of 1989, British housing stock was worth £1,000 billion, but just one year later £100 billion of this had evaporated. The struggle to meet mortgage payments was difficult for everyone, but particularly for those who had invested in 'buy to let' properties. Rents were high and home owners found that their mortgage payments didn't stretch far enough to fund buying a second home. The British public struggled, with the more unfortunate facing repossession and bankruptcy.

In response to the economic recession of 1990–91, when many people lost their jobs while mortgage rates peaked, the Government lowered interest rates. There was still £12 billion of negative equity among British home owners in 1993, but as interest rates fell and the economy recovered, the housing market revived again.

Despite the state of the housing market and warnings from experts that houses were for 'nesting not investing', large numbers of the public could not shake the psychological grip of home ownership. By 1996, confidence had returned to the housing market, demand rose and with it prices, with particularly sharp increases in central London.

HOME AFFORDABILITY

Housing Affordability Index (1992=100) and mortgage rates (%)

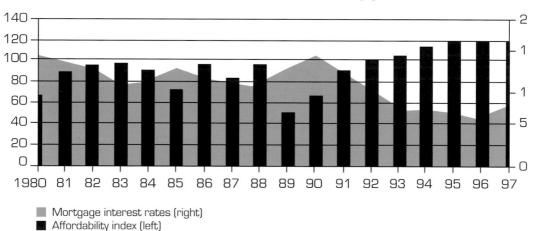

Mortgage interest rates (right)
Affordability index (left)

The housing market today

The sustained growth of house prices remained throughout the rest of the 1990s and into the 21st century. However, recent global events including September 11th and the war with Iraq have dented consumer confidence, and the general economic depression in the economy means that the market is slowing. It seems that the current economic and global climate, as well as the boom and bust of the 1980s/1990s property market, is causing nervousness among would-be buyers, while sellers still expect to receive predownturn prices. Many buyers are holding back, staying in their current property – even taking advantage of this slowing market to rennovate their properties – or renting until the market settles or, as they believe, becomes more realistic.

Interest rates are currently at 3.75% and have been voted to stay that way at a recent meeting of the Bank of England's Monetary Policy Committee. However, there are experts forecasting a dip in the property market, with some of them surmising the low point may be in 2005. Yet, as we know, there are no certainties in the buying and selling of houses. If we were to take the last 30 years as a guide, cyclically it would seem logical to suppose that the next pile of money to be made will come from buying stocks and shares, while we wait for the value to rise. But then all of you who like spending your weekends shovelling cement would be bored to tears!

If property is your passion then, regardless of whether it is the area to make the most money, you should stick with it. This book is more important than ever before because of this uncertain market. If you want to invest in property then you need to be confident that you're fully informed and able to make the right decisions. Use this book to expand your knowledge – it is your friend and advisor when the television series is no longer at hand.

Sarah Beeny
October 2003

HOW TO GET ON THE PROPERTY LADDER

THE PRACTICALITIES OF BUYING

Where to start

According to the Survey of English Housing, in 2002 70% of households in England owned their own homes. So how do you go about getting on the property ladder?

If you are a first-time buyer, finding a property and financing a sale can seem like a gargantuan task. If you have owned a home before but are looking for another, trying to discover all of the options available to you can be just as exhausting. Whatever your situation, the idea of legal documents, large sums of cash and red tape may seem daunting. This chapter will help demystify the terms and show you all the options so that you can decide which path to take.

Before you start looking at properties, think carefully about what you can afford. The general rule is that you can secure a mortgage of up to three and a half times your annual income. Look carefully at your finances, calculate the approximate monthly repayments you would need to make on a mortgage of this size and get advice from your accountant or bank manager if necessary. Next, approach several different mortgage lenders and see how much they will let you borrow and what types of mortgage are available. Remember to request a written 'offer in principle' to confirm the loan amount and terms. This will give you an indication of what you can spend and the paperwork may help when you are negotiating an offer. For the sake of your cash flow, many a good nights' sleep and securing a good deal, don't be tempted to look too far outside your price range.

SARAH SUGGESTS …

'Be strict with yourself, set an upper limit on what you can afford and stick to it. Don't let estate agents tempt you to overstretch yourself by luring you to look at more expensive properties unless they are confident that the vendor would consider a lower offer than the asking price.'

SEE ALSO

| Finding the right mortgage | p 22 |
| Additional costs of buying property | p 51 |

In addition, be aware that as well as your deposit, there are other costs involved when you buy property. These include stamp duty, lender's fees, land registry costs, legal fees and survey costs, as well as extras such as cash for buildings insurance, moving costs and VAT.

Finding the right property

Registering with estate agents is the obvious place to start your property hunting, but it is not the only option.

If you are prepared to do some research yourself, there are other ways of purchasing property, which can sometimes work out cheaper. From scouring the press for private sales to bidding at auctions, there are various ways to purchase property and each has its advantages as well as pitfalls. Once you have decided how you are going to find your property, take a good look at what is available. Get out there and get viewing!

Using estate agents

Begin by looking at agents' websites and local newspapers to compare prices and get a good feel for the property market in the area in which you wish to buy. Contact several estate agents in the area and register your details with them. It is a free service to be put on to their mailing lists and they should contact you as soon as they find a property that matches your requirements. In addition:

- Check your agents' websites regularly to inspect properties via a 'virtual tour' so that you don't waste time viewing in person unnecessarily.
- Telephone the branch regularly for updates or to ask for details of new properties on the market to ensure that your agent doesn't forget about you.
- When you go for viewings, be punctual and polite and strive to build up a good working relationship with your agent – you want them to call you as soon as a suitable property comes on to their books.

pros and cons

Estate agents have a very good understanding of the market and their area as they are aware of how the market is moving on a day-to-day basis. In addition, they can negotiate and mediate with the vendor on your behalf.

Buying privately

Once you have registered with agents, scoured the property press and are familiar with the property market, you could look in the small ads and on the internet for private sales.

pros and cons

Buying privately could save you a few thousand pounds if the vendor is advertising a property for a quick sale and deducts their saving in agents' fees from the asking price, but don't assume that a private sale is automatically a bargain. The disadvantages are that it is *you* who will be working for any financial saving. You may waste time viewing properties that are unrealistically described and will need to deal with the vendor directly. If you decide to pursue a private sale be sure you are clear about what you expect to be included in the sale and confirm any verbal agreements in writing.

PROPERTY POINTER ...

'Use a camcorder or digital camera if you have one to record your viewings as no amount of memory work compares with watching your tour again when you get home, but always seek permission from the vendors first.'

Buying off-plan

To buy off-plan is to buy a property that is yet to be built. This is a popular option for first-time buyers looking for competitively priced apartments in major cities. The best way to find out about new developments before they happen is through the property press.

Contact developers to see computer graphics and artist's impressions of the finished scheme and find out about their previous projects. Visiting these will give you a feel for the developer's design.

Make sure you have a full list of agreed internal fixtures and fittings from the developer in writing.

pros and cons

Buying early on in the development will allow you to 'cherry pick' the layout and view you like best. You can get a good deal – the developer usually asks for a reservation fee when you choose your apartment so they can show their financier they have a certain number of sales. This in turn frees up their cash flow and allows developers to offer the property at a price that is cheaper than when the scheme is complete. If the market is good, this often means that your investment has increased before you move in.

You may also benefit from the discounted deals your developer can take advantage of for fittings and furnishings for new constructions. These are often in the latest trends, which also add value to the property. Furthermore, if you manage to buy in a new development in an up-and-coming area, you could also be investing where prices are about to rise.

The disadvantage is that if the market drops, you are obliged to complete on the apartment at the same purchase price.

SEE ALSO

How to spot an   p 42
up-and-coming area

Buying at auction

Buying at auction can be another way to purchase property competitively. But be warned, there is much more to this method of buying than turning up and landing a bargain at the drop of the hammer. If you are not careful or have not been to an auction before, you could get carried away and end up bidding over the odds for a property.

You must do your research. Find out as much as possible about the property you are interested in bidding for well in advance of the auction day, and visit an auction house and sit in on a few property lots before you actually go to buy so that you understand how auctions work. You can find out where and when property auctions are held in your area from the local press or the internet.

> **SARAH SUGGESTS …** 'Auction houses are exciting places to be and it is easy to get carried away. Always have a top price at the forefront of your mind and stick to it. If the bidding gets too high, stop, think and if necessary give up.'

pros and cons

Although it is unlikely, if no one else at the auction shows an interest in the property you may be able to pick up a real bargain. However, buying at auction can be risky as they often sell run-down properties that require major structural work. If you buy on a whim, you can end up paying over the odds for a property. There is no room for error. Once the hammer goes down you are legally obliged to buy the property and you must complete within four weeks.

Other avenues

There are other ways to find cheap properties:
- Buy ex-council – look for brick-built properties, with roofs and windows in good condition and lots of private homes nearby.
- Look outside the peak periods of spring and autumn.
- Consider repossessions. Such properties may be in poor repair, but the mortgage lender will be keen to sell as quickly as possible and so a cheaper price may be negotiable (although the law says that lenders must get the 'best price reasonably obtainable').

How to spot a good buy

It may sound like a contradiction, but the best way of spotting a good buy is to avoid a bad one!

If you have done your research and viewed at least ten properties, you'll know whether the property is fairly priced, whether the asking price is a good reflection of the standard and size of accommodation on offer and the location of the property is to your liking.

You can also decide whether the pros outweigh the cons. My advice is to write out a mental wish list of all the things you realistically should be able to expect for your money, then see how the property matches up. There is normally a question of compromise. Be wary of properties on busy roads, flats in basements and taking on big DIY projects, for example, but remember that sometimes these elements mean value for money. It is all about striking the appropriate balance for you.

You need to assess how much work a property will need to turn it into a home. If your property has met all of the above criteria on your first viewing, then it is time for a second visit. Use this opportunity to take a good look at the structure and condition of the property. It is always worth taking along a parent or friend for a second opinion, especially if they have experience of buying or renovating a property. Remember to:

1 **Inspect the exterior of the property carefully.** Stand well back from the house. Look to see whether it is horizontally and vertically correct, whether the windows are level and whether there are any major cracks in the brickwork, particularly under windows. These are all possible indicators of subsidence or structural instability. Once inside, check for large cracks in the plasterwork, which is another clue to movement, although this may be historic. Now inspect the roof. Look for loose slates, worn-out tiles, unsound flashing or guttering.

2 **Check for signs of damp.** Can you spot any damp patches or musty smells in the property? Do the floorboards feel spongy as you walk around? Can you see any fungus or spores lurking in dark corners? Are there any wet patches on the walls or ceilings?

3 **Decide whether the property has been cared for.** If you feel that it has, the current owners are more likely to have fixed a problem, instead of allowing it to worsen. Look for signs of bad DIY jobs, poor finishes or attempts to mask problems. A house that has had TLC is often a better buy.

4 **Look for expensive elements that need updating.** After structural repairs and roofing these are most likely to be new windows, kitchen and bathroom suites and flooring.

5 **Check on the services.** Ask about the plumbing, check the age and condition of the boiler and when the house was last rewired.

SEE ALSO

The survey   p 26

SARAH SUGGESTS ... 'If a house has structural problems, don't panic, just be aware of the problem, be prepared to fix it immediately if you decide to make this your purchase and be sure the work that needs doing is reflected in the asking price.'

Leasehold and freehold

Is the property you've seen leasehold or freehold? It is important that you know the difference.

Freehold

If you are buying a house, it is likely to be freehold. This means that you legally own and are responsible for the house and its grounds. As such, it is your job to maintain the property and check the professional status of any workmen you employ to carry out repairs. You will need to be aware of any bylaws that may govern what you do, for example whether the property is in a conservation area, or whether it is a listed building. In multiple occupancy properties the residents may join together and purchase the freehold to ensure the property is well cared for.

Leasehold

Most flats are sold on a leasehold basis. This means you have bought a lease, which allows you to live in the property for a certain length of time. The actual owner of the building is the person or company who owns the freehold and you will have to pay them an annual ground rent. They are then responsible for ensuring the maintenance and upkeep of the building is carried out. For this service they will expect you to pay additional service charges for which they will arrange buildings insurance, cleaning and general maintenance. Any actual cost of extra works such as redecoration of communal areas or roof repairs will usually be split between the number of lease-holders in the building. On rare occasions, leaseholders may be responsible for all of the maintenance work on the property. Be sure to find out the details of the lease at the viewing stage. Always know what you are buying before you invest.

As with shortlease landlords, there are good and bad freeholders, some more responsible than others. If you have problems with shoddy work, inflated bills and poor management, you can get together with the other leaseholders in your block and present a case to your local leasehold valuation tribunal, a body that deals with disputes over service charges and the purchase of leasehold property by tenants holding long leases.

SARAH SUGGESTS …

'If the freeholder appears to have been less than diligent it is worth checking whether it is possible to buy out the freeholder or, alternatively, purchase a share of the freehold. This usually happens when all of the leaseholders have got together and formed a company to buy out the freeholder, transferring the responsibilities of the property to the parties who live there and giving them direct control of the property and its maintenance.'

CROUCH END
JOINT VENTURE

A joint purchase certainly worked for Katie Basham and her father. Katie was a first-time buyer in her late 20s who was desperate to get on the property ladder but found that London prices were beyond her reach. Her solution was to split the purchase 50/50 with her dad, who saw the proposition as a financial investment. He bought his share outright and Katie committed to a mortgage.

With her father's help, she decided to tackle a run-down five-bedroom maisonette in London's Crouch End with the idea of creating a flat share. Katie planned to live in one of the rooms and let out the others for a total income of £400 a week. Katie's half of the income would then cover her mortgage and running costs.

see page 127
for more on Katie's project

Funding your purchase

Now you have found out about every aspect of the property you are interested in, it is time to decide how you will fund your purchase.

As house prices have reached new heights, many first-time buyers have really struggled to purchase their own home. However, there are three ways of getting on the property ladder without too much difficulty. The first is to find the right mortgage for your financial situation, the second involves splitting the cost of a mortgage with another party and the third means applying for a government or council scheme.

Finding the right mortgage

With interest rates currently at their lowest for 30 years, mortgages are a competitive business for lenders and there are plenty of options on offer. Broadly speaking, there are two types of mortgages: interest-only and repayment mortgages, with variants of both on the market. Before you commit to any type of mortgage make sure you understand the technical terms and are aware of the implications that each deal could have for you:

1 **Interest-only mortgages.** With an interest-only mortgage your monthly payments to the lender cover only the interest on the loan. The full amount of the loan, i.e. the capital and the interest, have to be paid back to the lender by the end of the mortgage term. To do this most people with an interest-only mortgage invest additional money each month into an alternative savings fund with the expectation that it will grow enough to enable them to repay the loan at the end of the term.

   An endowment mortgage is where you pay only interest but you have an endowment policy set up in conjunction with the mortgage. Over a 25-year period, you would hopefully accrue a sufficient amount to pay off the outstanding capital. ISA mortgages and pension mortgages work on the same principles. They are all variations on the interest-only mortgage.

2 **Repayment mortgages.** With a repayment mortgage your monthly repayments cover both the capital and the interest on the loan. No other way of repaying the mortgage is needed although your lender might insist on life insurance in case you die before the mortgage is paid off. See the table on pages 24–5 for the different types of repayment mortgage available.

Buying together

If you cannot afford to invest in a property on your own, then buying jointly with someone else allows you to increase your borrowing power in a joint mortgage. Theoretically, you can apply for a joint mortgage for up to four people, although most lenders base their calculations for a loan on the incomes of two. As with a normal loan, they base the amount on three and a half times the main income, then add one of the secondary incomes to the equation.

If you don't want to opt for a joint mortgage, there are other ways of splitting the costs. A parent or family member may be willing to act as a guarantor on your loan. If so, it is important that all parties realise the implication – that the guarantor becomes liable for the loan in its entirety should your payments slide.

If you do buy with a second party, it is essential to have an agreement drawn up by a solicitor. This should state how much each party is contributing in terms of the deposit and mortgage repayments. It should also state the course of action to be taken if one owner wishes to leave or sell the property. Your agreement will then protect you and the other party from arguments in the event of a sale.

Government and council schemes

If you cannot afford a mortgage, consider some of the government schemes designed to help all but developers get on the property ladder. The Government recognises that the majority of people in the UK aspire to own their own home and has set up several schemes to assist those struggling to do so.

right to buy

Introduced in 1980, the 'Right to Buy' scheme still coincides with the aim of a recent Housing Green Paper, 'Quality and Choice, A Decent Home for All'. It allows council tenants of two years to purchase their own homes at a discounted price and, to date, has helped over 1.3 million council tenants in England buy their own homes. There are two options available under the 'Right to Buy'. Firstly, you can buy your home by paying the full purchase price with discounts ranging from 32 to 70% according to the number of years you have spent living there as a council tenant and subject to a maximum discount limit for the area in which you live. Secondly, you can use the 'Rent to Mortgage' scheme if you want to buy your home but cannot afford to pay for it all at once.

TIP

Note that government and council schemes are not open to property developers.

other schemes

There are some other low-cost home ownership schemes available:
- 'Right to Acquire' – a similar scheme, giving certain tenants of Registered Social Landlords (RSLs) a statutory right to buy their home at a discount.
- Homebuy – enables RSL and local authority tenants to buy a home on the open market with the help of an interest-free equity loan equal to 25% of the purchase price.
- Conventional Shared Ownership – allows RSLs to build, purchase and renovate existing dwellings for sale on shared ownership terms. The purchaser buys a share of a property and pays rent on the remaining share.
- Cash Incentive Scheme – aims to release local authority accommodation for letting to those in need of housing and encourages owner occupation. The scheme works by paying a grant to a tenant to help them buy a property in the private sector.
- Do-It-Yourself Shared Ownership – offered by a few local authorities, this allows people on low incomes access to home ownership. Unlike 'Conventional Shared Ownership', it allows a purchaser to select a property on the open market and then buy it on shared ownership terms, paying rent on the share they do not own.
- Starter Home Initiative – helps key workers on low incomes (such as health workers, teachers and the police) purchase a house in highly priced areas which are undermining recruitment in their sector.

DIFFERENT TYPES OF REPAYMENT MORTGAGE

REPAYMENT MORTGAGE TYPE	ADVANTAGES	DISADVANTAGES
Australian mortgage Still relatively unknown in the UK despite its introduction a couple of years ago. Allows people to pay their mortgage weekly and gives them a greater degree of flexibility.	Beneficial if you get paid weekly.	In the British market not many people wish to pay their mortgages on a weekly basis. (You can still get Australian mortgages but they are fading fast from the marketplace.)
Offset and current accounts Triggered by the less popular Australian mortgage (see above). As the interest rates on savings are currently at a low, using savings to pay less interest on a mortgage has become popular.	The rates are not that superior to normal fixed-rate or discounted mortgages but this type of mortgage lets you use your savings to pay off your mortgage and reduce the interest you pay. For example, if you have a £100,000 mortgage and £40,000 savings you can put that into the account. Offsetting £40,000 against the £100,000 means you pay interest on only £60,000.	If you can offset only £5,000, however, you are better choosing a normal fixed-rate or discounted mortgage at a lower rate as your payments would be much cheaper despite the offsetting.
Fixed-rate mortgage Probably the most popular type of mortgage.	Allows you to budget and provides protection against interest rate increases. Easy to understand and generally extremely competitive. Five- and two-year rates are excellent at the moment.	There can be high set-up fees. You are tied in with a redemption penalty so you cannot change your mortgage or take advantage of the interest rates if they fall. However, these disadvantages are relatively minor.
Discounted mortgage Very popular in the last two years while interest rates have been falling. Not too dissimilar to fixed-rate mortgages in terms of pricing.	Competitive in a market where interest rates are coming down as you can take full advantage of them being reduced.	No rate protection. If rates increase and you are tied in, most discounted mortgages have redemption penalties and, like the fixed-rate mortgages, you are trapped.
Capped-rate mortgage Like a fixed-rate and discounted mortgage rolled into one. With capped-rate mortgages people are often unaware that the rate that comes down follows the lender's standard variable rate (SVR) and not Bank of England base rate, which is currently on 3.75% while most lenders are on 5.5%+. So a capped-rate mortgage for 3.99% is really a two-year fixed-rate mortgage, because interest rates are unlikely to go below the SVR, which is unlikely to go below 4%.°	Good value for money if rates are falling; if rates are increasing you are protected and can still budget, as with a fixed-rate mortgage. For example, if you are capped at 5% and interest rates go up to 6%, your mortgage will never go higher than 5%. If interest rates fall below 5% you can take advantage of the interest rate coming down. Extremely beneficial in the last couple of years as interest rates have come down.	The interest is slightly higher than fixed-rate or discounted mortgages and, because it is unlikely that we will see lenders' SVR falling like they have over the last couple of years, you are not going to feel the advantage.

REPAYMENT MORTGAGE TYPE	ADVANTAGES	DISADVANTAGES

Tracker mortgage
Mirrors the Bank of England base rate. For example, if you had a Bank of England tracker at 6% a couple of years ago, you will have seen it come down now to 3.75%. To see the interest rate drop by 2.25% is great value.
	The Bank of England Committee meet monthly to decide what to do with the base rate, and produce the result on the first Thursday of each month. You might therefore have your interest rate cut each month with immediate effect if you have a Bank of England base rate tracker mortgage.	If the Committee decides to increase the rates every month and your mortgage has a redemption penalty (as most of them do) then you could see your mortgage repayment increasing every month and you will be stuck unless you pay the redemption and get out.
		   Most tracker mortgages don't exactly mirror the Bank of England base rate. Normally you are offered Bank of England base rate plus or minus 0.5%, but the pricing works out similar to fixed-rate and discounted mortgages in terms of the interest rate.
		   There is no rate protection whatsoever as tracker mortgages are immediately affected by changes in the Bank of England base rate.

Cashback mortgage From the mid 1990s Abbey National brought out a 95% mortgage, which gave you 5% cashback and meant you didn't need a deposit to buy property. Almost obsolete now that 100% mortgages are available.	Provides you with a cash lump sum, and enables you to buy property with no capital.	Normally on standard variable rate (SVR); no rate protection and if you want to pay off the mortgage early you have to pay back the full cashback.
100% mortgage Extremely popular in today's market as more and more people stretch their incomes.	Negates the need for a deposit and gets you on the property ladder. With a 100% mortgage if the market goes up and your property rises in value by 10% in the first year then you have accrued some equity in your property and made some money on it. Interest rates are not prohibitively high. For example 4.99% for a two-year fix with Northern Rock is not a great interest rate, but for 100% lending it is not too bad at all.	A 'high loan to value'. This means that with a 100% mortgage the value of the loan is equivalent to the value of the property so there is a higher risk of negative equity should house prices fall. Most lenders who lend over 90% therefore charge a mortgage indemnity premium and certainly those lending 100% charge quite a high percentage in this premium because of the risk involved to them. Look for the few lenders who do not charge for the deal, as well as those offering up to 125% mortgages. If the housing market starts to come down you could be in trouble and experience negative equity.

The survey

Once you have secured your mortgage, put in an offer for the property and got your solicitor on board, it is time to get serious about a survey.

Surveys are designed to give you the information you need to make an informed and sensible property purchase. The Consumer's Association and the Council of Mortgage Lenders both advise you to arrange a survey before buying a property. I advocate the same. When money is tight, the idea of spending more than the bare minimum may not be desirable, but a survey is essential if you are buying an old property or one that needs any degree of renovation. Do not rely on just a valuation.

TIP

Do not be tempted to skip having a survey done on your property as it might well uncover major problems in your project. Unless you are very experienced it is always wise to pay for a full survey and take professional building advice.

A valuation

A valuation, or 'basic valuation' as it is often called, is an inspection carried out on behalf of your mortgage lender to ensure their investment is sound. In other words, its purpose is to check that your intended property is worth at least the amount they are lending you and to identify any problems that could affect the security of the loan. Your mortgage lender will expect you to pay for the valuation. In addition to the cost of the valuation itself, you may also be charged an administration, or arrangement, fee by your bank or building society. You are entitled to know the amount of the fee being paid to the surveyor and the amount being retained by the lender.

A valuation is *not* a survey. It is a limited inspection. A property can have defects that are not of concern to the mortgage lender and therefore won't appear in a valuation report. Furthermore, a valuation does not provide you with any legal recourse as it is for the benefit of the lender only.

One of the biggest mistakes made by first-time buyers is to rely on the information provided by the valuation when deciding whether or not to purchase a property. Before you dismiss the idea of a survey, remember that they do give you a certain amount of legal recourse and are conducted for the benefit of the borrower rather than the lender.

Flat or Homebuyer's Survey and Valuation Report

The Homebuyer's Survey and Valuation Report (HSV) is a service carried out to a standard format defined by the Royal Institution of Chartered Surveyors (RICS). The HSV is primarily designed for properties built within the last 150 years, which are of conventional construction and in reasonable condition. An HSV does give you legal recourse but is not a detailed survey of every aspect of the property. It focuses only on significant and urgent matters.

An HSV seeks information on the following:
- The property's general condition.
- Urgent and significant matters that need assessing before entering into exchanging contracts (or before making an offer in Scotland), including recommendations for any further specialist inspections.

- Any significant defects in accessible parts of the property, which may affect its value.
- Results of any testing of walls for dampness.
- General comments on damage to timbers, including woodworm or rot and evidence of damp.
- Comments on the existence and condition of damp-proofing, insulation and drainage (although the latter will not be tested).
- The recommended reinstatement cost for insurance purposes. This means the anticipated costs of reconstructing a building in the event of its damage by an insured risk such as fire. It is not the same as the market value of the property.
- The value of the property on the open market.

Full structural, or building, survey

This is an in-depth and comprehensive inspection suitable for all properties but especially recommended for the following buildings:

A building survey can be as in-depth as you want and can be tailor-made to suit you and your property, but generally includes the following:

- All major and minor faults.
- The implications of any defects and probable cost of repairs.
- Results of testing walls for dampness and testing timbers for damage including woodworm or rot.
- Comments on the existence and condition of damp-proofing, insulation and drainage (although the latter will not be tested).
- Extensive technical information on the construction of the property and details of the materials used.
- Information on the location.
- Recommendations for any further specialist inspections.

Make sure you fully understand what is and isn't included in the survey. If you choose to instruct your own independent surveyor, ask about any specific information you would like to know before the survey is conducted, for example whether or not it will be feasible to make structural alterations. You should also mention any specific areas for investigation, such as testing the drains or checking for woodworm. If your surveyor isn't qualified to do this, he or she should be able to arrange for another specialist to do so.

Surveyors should comment on all parts of a property that are readily accessible but they are not obliged to inspect areas that are difficult to access. They won't lift carpets, shift furniture, use a ladder to inspect the roof or move items stored in the loft unless you specifically instruct them to do so. Similarly, since most surveyors are not trained electricians or plumbers, they will not test services such as the wiring and water supply. However, they may comment on their condition. Where necessary, surveyors will recommend that an expert examination be carried out.

Read the terms and conditions of the survey carefully and double-check with your surveyor if you are unclear about anything. Use the results of your survey to make a reasoned and informed judgement as to whether or not to proceed with the purchase, and to assess whether or not the property is a reasonable purchase at the agreed price. Be clear what decisions and courses of action should be taken *before* the contracts are exchanged.

How to find a surveyor

You may find that your mortgage lender or estate agent can recommend a surveyor. It is worth asking whether they have a working relationship with one. You can check by the letters after the surveyor's name – MRICS or FRICS – whether they are a professional member and fellow of the Royal Institute of Chartered Surveyors (RICS) – or TechRICS for technical surveyors. If you do not have a recommendation, contact the RICS directly. RICS members are qualified, experienced and have to give impartial advice. They also carry their own professional indemnity insurance.

SEE ALSO

Resources   p 154

CASE STUDY

Neath: Breaking the rules

At just 23, Kim Maoate decided to give up her IT job and pursue a career in property development. For her first project she bought a three-bedroom Victorian terraced house in Neath, Wales, near the town centre.

PROJECT COSTS

Cost of property	£27,500
Renovation budget	£11,500
Target resale price	£52,000
Anticipated pre-tax profit	**£13,000**

the plan

Kim planned to work on the property full time and gave herself eight weeks for the renovation. One reason for the short schedule was because Kim lives in Buckinghamshire. She planned to stay in a B&B in Neath while the messy work was done and then move into the property when it became habitable. She estimated this would be just two weeks into the project. Considering the state of the property, I hoped she was being realistic.

This terraced house was dark, damp and in a very bad state of repair. Every room needed work doing to it. Built in an extension downstairs was a bathroom, which would need to be moved upstairs. This would be a tricky job, requiring a macerator instead of replumbing. The property had only one other outside loo, which Kim planned to move into a downstairs cupboard. It also had a dilapidated lean-to, which also needed to be knocked down. Kim planned to create a patio area in its place and lay the paving stones herself.

Kim's house also needed rewiring, new windows, central heating and total redecoration. The ceilings were cracked and the floorboards were rotten The master bedroom had a huge hole in the ceiling where the roof had been leaking and needed urgent repair. Kim took inspiration from the hole and, turning a negative into a positive, wanted to repair the damage and make the hole into a loft access.

sarah's advice

This appeared to be a complicated first development project, with a lot of work to be done in a short schedule and on a tight budget. I wondered why Kim had chosen to take on such a big project and a house that needed so much work. Kim explained that she had bought the property without ever seeing it. She was pretty horrified to discover what she had been planning to invest in when she visited the house for the first time with her own set of keys. She found out that the property was next door to a boarded-up house and the interior was in an appalling state. I was therefore glad to hear that Kim had instructed a survey. But, despite the property being over 100 years old with visible damp, leaks and cracks, she had opted for only a Homebuyer's Survey, and being so inexperienced she was unable to asses the real damage and the investment that would need to be made to get the property up to scratch.

The survey mentioned 'evidence of woodworm infestation', but Kim had no money in her budget to get it treated. When she started to rip off the wallpaper, she discovered that all the plaster beneath was unsound and would need to be hacked off the walls – a mammoth task.

I started to fear for Kim's tiny budget. I soon found out that she had based some of her figures on guesswork rather than real quotes. She had spent time researching the decorating and garden costs, but had neglected to price the building work, plumbing and electrical jobs, which were so important. By neglecting to calculate her budget accurately, Kim was already losing sight of her profit.

The other area Kim overlooked was her target market. She didn't seem to know who she was marketing the property to. She aimed to do up the property simply so that it had mass appeal and was suitable for both first-time buyers as well as the elderly. I was concerned that by doing this, she would give mixed signals to

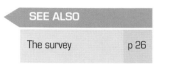

SEE ALSO

The survey   p 26

prospective buyers who would feel that certain elements could have been more in tune with their lifestyles.

Kim broke most of the rules of buying a property for development. She hadn't seen the property or the area before she made an offer and had failed to have an appropriate survey on a property that desperately needed one and didn't research or calculate a realistic budget for the job.

She had to work really hard at getting the most out of the property by getting a grip on her budget, getting the work done properly and hoping for a lot of luck.

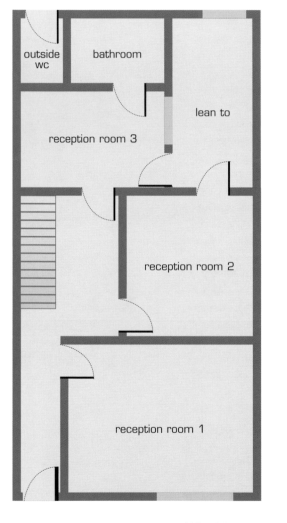

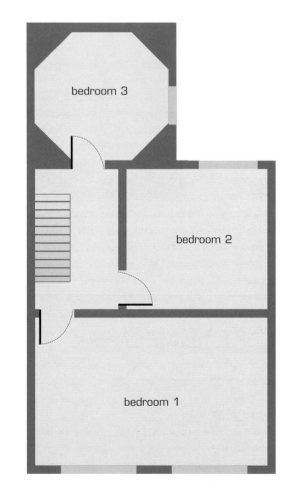

When Kim bought this Victorian terrace there was just one bathroom downstairs, built in a lean-to and an outside WC. Kim planned to knock down the dilapidated extension, move the bathroom upstairs to the master bedroom with the help of a macerator and relocate the downstairs loo to a cupboard. A property with just one bathroom and no separate WC is often unattractive to buyers, so while I saw Kim's logic, I wondered if the macerator would be an even bigger turn-off.

Buying property in Scotland and Ireland

The property buying process varies all over the world. This chapter has focused on purchasing in England and Wales, but the rules differ in Scotland and Ireland.

Wherever you intend to buy a home or a property to develop, make sure you understand the basic property laws and systems of the country to make your purchase less stressful than necessary.

Buying in Scotland

In Scotland, most properties are sold through solicitors rather than estate agents, although estate agencies have become increasingly commonplace in recent years. Solicitors are able to call themselves 'Solicitors and Estate Agents' and some set up 'Solicitors' Property Centres', where details of all properties being sold by solicitors in the area can be found. The centres are financed by subscriptions from the member solicitors and by charges made to sellers of property – as in the UK, the service is free to prospective buyers. Other solicitors' firms have their own property department and employ sales staff to deal with the non-legal aspects of buying and selling in these offices.

A list of buildings for sale in Scotland with historical or architectural importance is issued quarterly by The Historic Buildings Bureau for Scotland, while all types of properties are widely advertised in the Scottish press and on the internet for sale.

In Scotland, if you are interested in buying a property you have seen at a property centre or a solicitor's you will be directed to the solicitor actually selling it. You will also need a solicitor for conveyancing. English solicitors are not able to practise in Scotland, so if you are relocating from outside Scotland, ask your usual solicitor whether they have a Scottish contact or recommendation. The Law Society of Scotland also produces a 'Directory of General Services', listing the contact details of practising solicitors throughout Scotland, as well as brochures detailing all of the relevant procedures and legalities. Be warned, there is no scale of solicitors' fees in Scotland – you will have to shop around to get a competitive estimate.

property pricing

The way that property is priced for scale in Scotland is unique. Generally, properties are presented for sale at 'offers over' a stated figure. Depending on demand for a property, the price eventually paid may be considerably higher than the original figure; it is rare for a purchaser to pay the asking price or below it. Sometimes properties are offered at a fixed price, usually because the owner wants a quick sale or the property hasn't sold at an 'offers over' price. In this instance a buyer should be ready to proceed very quickly, as the first acceptable offer at the stated price will secure the property.

surveys and making an offer

When you tell your solicitor that you are interested in buying a particular property he will telephone the seller's solicitor or estate agent to register your interest. The seller's solicitor or estate agent will then give you a chance to offer for the property although he is not legally obliged to.

The process of obtaining a mortgage in Scotland is similar to that in England and most of the major English banks and building societies and all the Scottish banks will lend on the security of Scottish properties. As the buying process can move very quickly in Scotland you would be wise to make sure the necessary loan finance will be available when you need it – subject always to a satisfactory survey on the chosen property.

However, in Scotland it is usual to have a survey carried out before you make an offer for a property. If your offer is accepted you are bound to proceed with the purchase and it is too late to discover defects or that you cannot get a loan on the property. This does mean that if your offer is unsuccessful you will have wasted the survey fee. Your solicitor will usually instruct that the survey takes place once you have told him you are interested in buying the property.

If you are happy with the surveyor's report, the next thing to do is to make an offer – usually through your solicitor. When making an offer you must specify all the conditions under which you want to buy the property and also how much you wish to pay. Prices quoted as 'offers over' usually mean another 10–15% on the price noted. Your solicitor will guide you on how much to offer – this is where a solicitor with knowledge of the local market is useful. In your offer you must also state when you want to move into the property, although this can be further negotiated with the seller at a later date.

acceptance of offer

In Scotland, once your offer has been accepted, the property is yours. When the details of the offer are sorted out between the two parties' solicitors, letters are exchanged between them, which create a legally binding contract. These are known in Scotland as the 'missives' and are the equivalent to the exchange of contracts in England and Wales. So, whether your offer is successful or not, you know where you stand very quickly. This is an advantage to the purchaser in the Scottish property buying system.

Once your solicitor has concluded the missives, the rest of the purchase goes through. Your solicitor will finish the conveyancing process and you will complete any loan application papers outstanding. Your solicitor will then meet the seller's solicitor and hand over a cheque for the full price in exchange for the title deeds, which he will then hand over to you.

If you buy in Scotland and intend to make the property your principal residence you will acquire Scottish domicile. It is advisable to consult a solicitor at this point, as it may affect, among other things, the way the property is inherited on your death.

SEE ALSO

Resources   p 154

Buying in Ireland

In Ireland the process of buying a property is slightly different to England and Wales. It is common to buy through an estate agent, privately or at an auction. Your solicitor obtains draft contracts and copy title from the seller's solicitors. The purchaser signs and returns the contract, along with a deposit (normally 10% of the purchase price), to be signed by the seller. As soon as these contracts have been signed by both parties and the deposit paid there is a binding agreement requiring the seller to hand over possession and you to hand over the balance on the closing date expressed in the contract.

Once a binding agreement is in existence a list of closing documents is set out, all of which must be handed over by the seller's solicitor in exchange for the balance.

Prior to closing the transaction your solicitor should make relevant enquiries to establish, for instance, there are no judgements affecting the property, no orders against the seller or any adverse registrations pending against the property.

Your solicitor normally attends at the offices of the seller's Solicitor with a Bank Draft for the balance. This will be handed over only when the closing documents are found to be in order and the Searches are found to be clear. You become the owner when the Bank Draft is exchanged for all these documents. Keys are then handed over and you can take possession.

SEE ALSO

| p 17 | Finding the right property |
| p 154 | Resources |

CHAPTER SUMMARY

1 Aside from your deposit, there are other costs involved in buying a property. Make sure you budget for every aspect of your purchase.

2 Estate agents are the obvious place to start hunting for property, but they are not the only option. Find out the best route for you.

3 Always remember your top price at an auction so you don't get carried away. Stop to think if the bidding gets too high and give up if necessary.

4 Reading about mortgage packages may not get your heart racing, but good research will help get you the best deal.

5 If you decide to buy a property with a friend or family member, always have a contract drawn up by a solicitor to protect both parties.

6 Remember, a valuation is *not* a survey. Neglect to have a survey carried out at your peril!

7 If your dream property has structural problems, make sure that: a) you know the full extent of the problem, b) you can fix it immediately and c) the property's asking price reflects the work that needs doing.

8 Wherever you buy property make sure you are familiar with the pertinent legal processes as these do vary from country to country.

BUYING
TO DEVELOP

Start thinking like a developer

There is a big difference between buying a new home and buying to make cash from bricks and mortar. It is easy to come unstuck if you confuse the two.

When you buy a home, you choose an area and type of house because you want to live there. You often invest all the money you have on making it the perfect place for you and your family's needs. All notions of budget go out of the window as you are investing in a home, and that has no price tag. You can indulge your creative passions and impose your own style. You leave odd jobs for years, save up to afford others because you have no particular schedule and adapt your home to suit any changes to your lifestyle. You do all of these things because home comes first and you are not selling for a profit. If, however, you are buying a property to develop you need to change your focus and fast. In short, you need to treat property development like a business if you want to make a business out of it.

THINK LIKE A DEVELOPER

- Find out whether there is a particular market for your end product or a high demand for a certain type of property in a certain area. The information in this chapter will help you decide on an area in which to invest and a narrower market to target within the broad one.
- Be objective about property. Abandon your own likes and dislikes and renovate for your market.
- Think of a property as a product.
- Renovate for maximum profit. Don't make expensive changes that may not be appreciated by a potential buyer. Don't renovate for personal taste; invest instead in creating a sound home for someone.
- Get organised. Don't forget that developing property means running a business.
- Be committed to budgeting. Remember, every penny you spend on a project makes a difference to your profit.
- Don't assume that just because a property needs modernising it is suitable to develop. Do your research and find out whether you can make money from the property.
- Be realistic about what you can take on. Use this book to help you decide when to get advice, when to get a helping hand with a project and when to DIY. Think carefully and realistically about the time and the energy you have to invest in a project before you commit to it.

SEE ALSO

Is it a deal?   p 50

Identifying your market

Like all businesses, property development works on the basis of supply and demand. It's about creating a desirable product for a prevalent market.

Know who your market is, understand what they want, target their needs accordingly and you will have the starting point for a successful development.

The market at large

As a general rule, aim to appeal to the broadest possible market. When considering a project put yourself in the shoes of as many different people – from all ages and all walks of life – as possible. Look carefully at the layout, location, size, style and facilities the property offers, as well as the amenities provided by the local area. The fewer elements in your completed property to which these groups can object, the greater will be the demand for your finished product. Of course, this also applies to how you renovate and decorate your property, which is explored in Chapter Five (see page 100).

Defining your target market

Having considered the market in general, focus on the actual market for whom you are aiming to develop your property. This specific and narrow sector is the group of people most likely to want to buy your property. To define and identify your market, think about what the property offers, who you could imagine living there and what they can afford. Use the table overleaf to help identify your market.

Once you have identified your market and know what your target buyers want, you can tailor your renovation plans to their needs and price range. However, you will often find that identifying your market and choosing an area come together at the same time.

SARAH SUGGESTS … 'The key to property developing is to appeal to the widest possible market without alienating your target market.'

SEE ALSO

p 40   How to decide on an area

IDENTIFYING YOUR TARGET MARKET

TARGET MARKET	WHAT THEY WANT	WHAT THEY DON'T WANT	PROPERTY OF MOST INTEREST TO THEM
First-time buyers	• Functional, utilitarian accommodation. • An up-and-coming area – usually in the centre of a town or city, with good facilities, recreation and travel links nearby.	• Plush fixtures and fittings that make the property cost a premium. This market is yet to make the cash to afford luxuries and will be happy with modern but basic furnishings. • A property that needs a lot of maintenance (so outside space is not necessary). • High service charges.	• A studio or self-contained one-bedroom flat, or larger apartment/small house with scope for sharing. Well-proportioned rooms – every bedroom has room for a double bed.
Professionals	• The luxury of space • High standards of fittings and finishes, and décor in cutting-edge style. • At least one bathroom to three bedrooms with a good shower and ideally a separate loo. • A space for eating and entertaining.	• A large garden. • To be near schools or stuck out in the sticks.	• A generously proportioned apartment with on-street parking in a desirable location, within walking distance of trendy. restaurants, bars, shops, delis and gyms, as well as travel links.
Young couples	• A house or maisonette with two or three bedrooms with room for the couple to grow into a family. • A garden. • A generous kitchen with eating area (for cooking family meals while watching young children and entertaining friends). • Plenty of storage space • A comfortable and practical living space. • Value for money.	• A galley kitchen with little space to manoeuvre. • A small master bedroom or reception room. • No outside space.	• A terraced or semi-detached house with a garden, near local schools, shops and amenities.

TARGET MARKET	WHAT THEY WANT	WHAT THEY DON'T WANT	PROPERTY OF MOST INTEREST TO THEM
Growing families	• A flexible layout that allows luxury, practicality and privacy. • High-spec design, luxurious but child-friendly fittings and finishes. • A large garden. • A separate bathroom for adults and children – children's bathroom a good size with a bath, not a shower. • Plenty of storage. • A garage and off-street parking.	• Open-plan living spaces. • Small reception rooms. • No outside space.	• A large house with potential, preferably near amenities and schools, but in a quiet residential area.
Retired people	• To downsize to a low-maintenance flat (ground floor or with a lift), bungalow or small house. • Practical, simple but comfortable designs with new, easy-to-use fittings and fixtures. • Large rooms that fit twin beds. • A communal garden or labour-free outside space, for example a small patio garden or balcony.	• Low level ovens and dishwashers. • Stiff locks; anything that needs to be updated or replaced in a few years' time. • Poor layout with long distances to walk. • To be isolated from others in a village, town or city.	• A compact one- or two-bedroom property with a layout that allows the dining area to be in or next to the kitchen, is near local shops and public transport, and has the potential to be pretty and practical.

How to decide on an area

You need to know an area well in order to invest in it and be confident you can make money there.

This means finding out about the amenities the area offers, how much property sells for, what kind of housing stock is available and who lives there. For this reason I often advise first-time developers to choose an area they know something about – primarily where they themselves, their friends or family live. Even when this is the case, the key to buying in the right location is research.

Become informed

Read the property press and local newspapers regularly. Look in estate agents' windows. Follow the performance of house sales in different areas to get an idea of what is selling and for how much. This way you will start to spot up-and-coming areas as well as good deals yourself, rather than relying on estate agents to tell you.

Use professional indexes and surveys to chart trends in the marketplace. Hometrack, for example, produces an independent property database by assessing the sale results of 3,500 estate agency offices covering 2,200 postcode districts in England and Wales. Similarly, Alliance & Leicester's 'movingimproving' index is a quarterly survey that pinpoints where in the UK people are currently buying homes, or areas to which people want to relocate. Surf the internet to find many more.

Visit the area

Once you have an informed interest about the property market in a specific area, visit it to see exactly what is on offer. The best way to discover all the information you need first-hand is to spend an afternoon there. So that you use your time efficiently, use the following checklists of positive and negative features when considering an area to develop in:

TIP

Green and open spaces are highly desirable, but only if they stay that way. Check whether they are protected environments by phoning the local council, or you may find the lovely field that your property overlooks turns into a retail park.

SEE ALSO

How to spot an up-and-coming area	p 42
Resources	p 154

CHECKLIST

THINGS TO BE NEAR

- ☐ Good schools
- ☐ Leisure and entertainment facilities
- ☐ Open or green spaces
- ☐ Quality shopping, high-street names, trendy bars
- ☐ Good transport links
- ☐ Well-maintained properties and gardens

THINGS TO AVOID

☐ Poorly rated schools

☐ Electricity pylons, mobile telephone and telecom masts, water or refuse station

☐ Areas dominated by noisy pubs, clubs and bars

☐ Areas (noisy and busy) close to a main road, railway track or under a flight path; areas known for traffic congestion or with poor transport links

☐ A derelict house

☐ Rough, badly maintained housing

☐ Evidence of poor council services, for example build-up of rubbish, graffiti, abandoned cars, dirty streets

ANOTHER EXPERT'S WORDS ...

A senior economist speculates that: 'Roads and railways are the biggest positive influences on the price of our homes, adding 10–11% to property values, but make sure communication links aren't too close. Being on a noisy road or right next to a railway line or under a flight path has a big negative impact; it can lop up to 15% off the value of your property.'

Use other resources

Of course you cannot find out everything about a village, town or city in one afternoon. Use the internet and telephone to gather more information on an area once you are at home:

- Use the internet to access the DfES (Department for Education and Skills) website and look up the School and College Performance Tables, or contact Ofsted (Office for Standards in Education).
- Similarly, check for local environmental issues by entering the postcode you are interested in on the Homecheck website or at the Environment Agency website.
- Do some thorough research on the region. Contact local newspapers, local councils and tourist boards. The One Account also offers free home buying guides for eleven regions in England.
- Visit the Up My Street website for information on local postcodes, property prices, local events and affairs and crime statistics, plus neighbourhood profiles on matters like average earnings, employment levels and preferred TV channels.
- Try out the transport links – call National Rail Enquiries for train timetable information or the Travel Line for details of local bus routes.
- Check out any potential developments in your area. Speak to the local council's planning department where all plans need to be lodged before they are approved.
- Speak to local groups such as Neighbourhood Watch or Round Table to see whether there are any issues or local flashpoints that your estate agent hasn't told you about.
- Check any noise levels, for example at pub closing time. Your solicitor will be able to find out for you whether there have been any official complaints lodged about noisy neighbours.

SEE ALSO

p 154   Resources

How to spot an up-and-coming area

We all dream of beating the competition to invest in a property in an up-and-coming area, but be warned. Areas predicted to be the next 'big thing' often take a while to mature and come into their own.

TIP

Remember, extensive commercial or large-scale housing developments can affect the atmosphere of an area and are not always seen as desirable by home hunters.

Play it safe and look out for businesses, groups and organisations who have already done the research and are currently investing. Look out for the following ten indicators:

1 A large chain of estate agents setting up new offices – this is a sign of a healthy or recently increased turnover of domestic property. You could even put in a call to ask about the supply and demand of property in that area.

2 The presence of major banks on the high street.

3 The opening of popular supermarket chains and off-licences.

4 The opening of luxury or specialist business such as delis, art galleries or wine merchants, all of which indicate an area of affluence.

5 New large-scale developments such as lofts and apartments, which indicate a response to high demand for housing. The type of housing being built will also tell you the target market.

6 Head offices, production plants or new divisions of major companies setting up in an area. A boom in employment will generate a demand for housing.

7 Evidence of council or government regeneration, improvements in transport links, plans for large-scale buildings or other such initiatives.

8 Local residents comprising smart, young business people and families; properties in good condition with well-tended gardens and façades.

9 The arrival of large-scale property developers in the area.

10 The renaming of a neighbourhood, for example 'Brackenbury Village' instead of just 'Hammersmith' will get people to think more highly of an area.

SARAH SUGGESTS …

'Look out for the ten up-and-coming-area indicators in a town or region containing a quantity of unmodernised housing. Many mid-income home hunters will buy in these areas, especially if they are in close proximity to an already affluent area in which they aspire to live.'

Swansea: Targeting the market

DIY enthusiasts Jo and Angela bought a dilapidated cottage on the outskirts of Swansea and planned to turn it into a family home. Property in the area was cheap, attracting a lot of first-time buyers and young families who could not afford the higher prices of the city. I recommended that Jo and Angela target these groups of buyers. If they renovated accordingly, they could ensure a sale quickly and at the right price.

PROJECT COSTS

Cost of property	£19,000
Renovation budget (including contingency)	£10,000
Target resale price	£45,000
Anticipated pre-tax profit	**£16,000**

Jo and Angela's cottage was in need of complete modernisation to make it habitable. It had no central heating, it needed rewiring and damp-proofing. More seriously, there was no proper kitchen or bathroom. At the front of the house was a small reception room, behind which a further room housed two cupboards, one containing a bath and a basin. At the rear of the building was a ramshackle extension – home to the only loo, a storage area and an unusable kitchen. This flimsy extension was tucked between the retaining wall of the garden and the house, blocking out all of the light and making the ground floor very dark. More importantly, it was suffering penetrating damp. There were three bedrooms upstairs, one at the front and two at the rear, both of which were level with the base of the steep, 100 foot-long back garden.

the plan

Jo and Angela gave themselves just fourteen weeks to develop the cottage and get it back on the market. To cut costs, they planned to do a lot of the DIY themselves. My first impression was that this was a huge project for such inexperienced developers, with all of their savings on the line. They broke down their budget as follows:

RENOVATION COSTS

Kitchen extension	£3,400
Modernisation (rewiring, etc.)	£2,000
Bathroom	£800
Decorating	£2,600
Contingencies	£1,200
Total renovation cost	**£10,000**

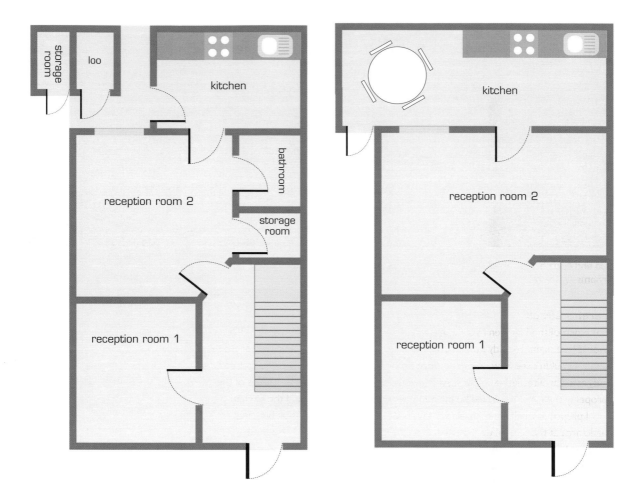

Jo and Angela planned on remodelling the original layout of their property. They wanted to rebuild the ramshackle extension at the back of the building to house a galley kitchen and create a larger reception room from the two downstairs cupboards. However, the rebuild would need to tackle the problems of building into the side of a hill and seemed ambitious on their budget.

Jo and Angela planned to install a new bathroom in one of the upstairs bedrooms. This did mean losing a bedroom, but most modern couples or young families prefer this arrangement and it would add value to the property. This also meant they could rip out the two downstairs cupboards and create a large reception room, demolish the old loo and kitchen and make one long galley kitchen. If you are changing the fundamental layout of a property, make sure that it will be appropriate for your market. Jo and Angela's plans were good though ambitious considering they had a budget of only £10,000. However, they seemed unaware of the potential complications of building into the side of the hill.

Jo and Angela maximised the living space in their cottage by knocking three tiny rooms into one.

sarah's advice

If the demolished kitchen extension was not properly rebuilt, the new galley kitchen would be a damp, mouldy hole that would show up on a survey and could jeopardise a sale. I couldn't see how doing the work properly was feasible on their budget, so I suggested an alternative solution, which would concentrate on the two areas of the property their market would be most interested in – the garden and the kitchen.

I proposed that Jo and Angela still knock down the flimsy extension but create a patio area at the back of the house, which would look attractive and also bring light into the back of the house. They could relocate the kitchen to the back reception room, using sliding doors to close it off when not in use and still use the front reception room as a living room. The benefits of this plan were that it kept to their original budget and created more light. But Jo and Angela went ahead with their original idea.

Jo and Angela installed a bathroom in one of the upstairs bedrooms. This did mean losing a bedroom, but is an arrangement their market often prefer.

I recommended an alternative solution, maximising on the garden and the kitchen – the two key areas of most interest to their intended market. If they knocked down the flimsy extension Jo and Angela could replace it with a patio area to create an outside eating area and bring light into the back of the house. They could then move the kitchen to the back reception room and insert sliding doors to close it off when not in use. This solution would add more light property and enable Jo and Angela to stick to their original budget.

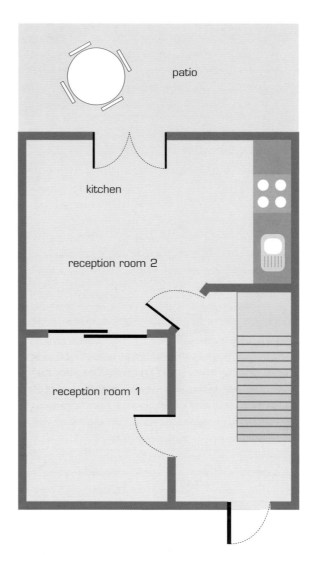

how the project progressed

Almost immediately, Jo and Angela's builder confirmed my fears regarding the serious problem with their plans for the kitchen extension. The back wall of the kitchen extension was only a single skin thick, just within the retaining wall of the garden. I was worried that this form of construction was in no way likely to be effective in the long term as a barrier against the penetrating moisture of the garden. They decided to hope for the best, demolish and rebuild the inner skin. The extension was built swiftly afterwards, but their original quote was already in trouble.

The damp problems did not stop there. A puddle of water appeared in the back reception room. The gradient of the garden and the fact that there was no effective drainage when it rained meant that water was running down from the garden and pooling through the cracks in the floor. They had no choice but to stop work and

SEE ALSO

p 54   Tip on contingency funds

deal with the problem. The damp travelled up from the floor to the plasterboard and up the wall in the reception room, while another puddle appeared a week later in their new kitchen extension. Having already plastered the walls, Jo and Angela had to dig up the floors in the back reception room and kitchen, lay a damp-proof membrane and new floors throughout. This, as you can imagine, diminished their contingency fund somewhat.

Jo and Angela now had to work very hard to stick to their budget as well as find more money to finish the project. Fortunately, a neighbour wanted to buy a small back section of their garden and was willing to pay £3,000 for it. The remaining garden would certainly be large enough for a two-bedroom house. Wisely, Jo and Angela decided to try not to plough the £3,000 back into their budget and still stick to their original costings.

Soon afterwards, a local skip company accidentally knocked down some of their front garden wall when removing a skip and promised to compensate. Jo and Angela decided to use the opportunity to apply for permission to knock the area flat and make a parking space, which would definitely add value to the property. The house stood on a busy main road and had no off-street parking. This was a lucky mishap, and I would always recommend you seize any such opportunity of making positive changes that will directly appeal to your market.

Back inside the house Jo and Angela concentrated on renovating the upstairs. They had budgeted for £800 to buy a new suite, fixtures and fittings for their new bathroom. I thought this needlessly extravagant for a house at this end of the market. I admired their ability to find a whole new bathroom suite for £400, but also felt they should have saved this money. They would have received the top selling price for the property without the added luxury of a power shower and could have recycled some of their original bathroom fittings by re-enamelling the bath and cleaning up the taps. You should invest only in areas that will add value to a property; in this instance the new bathroom did not.

Jo and Angela demolished the ramshackle extension and decided to rebuild it. They fitted a smart new kitchen, which would really help to sell the property.

Jo and Angela managed to claw back most of their unexpected overspends through scrimping in other areas. I was impressed by Jo and Angela's gritty determination to stay on schedule and within their budget despite all of their setbacks, but their rejigging of the budget left them very little money to finish the project. I feared that if they compromised in areas of decorating and finish, it would affect the standard of their overall product and ultimately the asking price. Here's how their final spend compared with their original budget:

SUMMARY OF RENOVATION COSTS

	ORIGINAL BUDGET	FINAL SUMS
Kitchen extension	£3,400	£5,000 (one-third more than planned)
Modernisation (rewiring, etc.)	£2,000	£3,950
Bathroom	£800	£821
Decorating	£2,600	£1,099
Contingencies	£1,200	
Total renovation cost	**£10,000**	**£10,870**

TIP

Start any necessary work in the garden as soon as possible so that new grass and other plants can look reasonably established by the time the property goes on the market.

With their decorating budget slashed, Jo and Angela found they were left with only £2,000 to buy and install a new kitchen (including all of the necessary appliances), buy and lay flooring throughout the property and tidy the garden.

Kitchens sell houses so it was important to get this right. The lack of light and space in Jo and Angela's kitchen made their task a difficult one. They decided to take advantage of a free kitchen design service at their local kitchen store.

Jo and Angela made great improvements to the exterior of their property. However, I wondered if a garden gate might give some extra privacy to the kitchen.

Armed with a design that maximised light and space, Jo and Angela hunted for the cheapest kitchen they could find. This type of development does not require an expensive bespoke kitchen and they managed to come in on budget. To do so Jo and Angela laid the tiles in this room and in the bathroom themselves. This was a brave decision as tiling is a skilled job and poor workmanship may put off potential buyers. The same principle relates to laying carpets – it is worth spending money to get the job done professionally. They also decided to sand and varnish the floorboards in the bedrooms themselves. This saved a bit of money in materials but their labour- and time-consuming work did not result in a perfect finish. Jo and Angela managed to save more money by using end-of-roll pieces of carpet which, while limiting the choice available, did keep costs down.

the outcome

Jo and Angela's priorities appeared to change when they started to run out of funds. They abandoned their idea for off-street parking and did not box in pipes or the boiler. Their wallpapering, paintwork and tiling was a little rushed. They left mowing the lawn a bit late and did little to improve the appearance of the garden. Estate agents who valued the property noticed the finishes were not too good.

Jo and Angela put their property on the market at £59,950, as property prices had risen between 15 and 20% in their area over the previous six months. However, the overall finish may have had an adverse affect on potential buyers. Jo and Angela ended up dropping the price and selling eight weeks later for £54,000. They had pinpointed the perfect area for their project, but if they had tailored their renovation more to their market's needs and had not cut so many corners, their development could have been even more successful. They did manage to stick close to their budget but if they had been more careful about the overall budget and market they could have made even more in terms of profit.

Is it a deal?

Now you have some ideas on how to target your market and identify your area, you need to know how to spot a deal. The simple answer lies in whether you can achieve a 20% profit margin? If you can then, *yes*, it is a deal!

Professional developers generally buy at a price that assures them a 20% gross return on their total investment. They do this to guarantee themselves a reasonable profit on their investment and protect themselves from movement in the market. I strongly recommend you try to do the same. Take a £100,000 flat, for example:

THE DEAL

Buy for	£100,000
Spend	£20,000
Sell for	£144,000
Make	**£24,000**

Be sure to work out your figures after viewing any property you are serious about. That way, you won't waste any time considering properties that are financial 'no gos'.

The most simple and comprehensive way to work out the maths is to subtract the associated fees and costs, renovation and purchase costs from the potential selling price of your property. *But*, to get to this stage you must calculate the following:

- The realistic resale value of the property.
- The cost of renovation works to the property.
- The sum total of all associated fees and costs you will incur during the project.

TIP
To determine the realistic resale value of your intended property, ask the estate agent for the actual sale price of a similar property rather than its asking price. The latter is merely the price the owner originally hoped to achieve.

The realistic resale value

What will your property be worth in peak condition? What are people willing to pay for newly renovated properties in your area?

Finding out the realistic resale value or 'ceiling price' of a property can tell you instantly whether it is a deal. It will guide you towards buying for the right price, reveal how much the property will be worth once it looks its best and help you work out your potential profit margin. So, before investing in a property, ensure that calculating its realistic resale value is your prime concern and most essential research:

- Build a profile of the property you are interested in. Be realistic and base your profile on the location, building type, number of rooms, features and layout of your property.
- Next, contact three local estate agents. Ask how much newly modernised properties of this profile have recently sold for in your area. See how the details of these properties match your profile.

• Calculate a realistic resale value from the comparables that closely match your profile. If the sale of a comparable property was completed more than two months ago, get an up-to-date opinion of what a newly renovated property of the same calibre would fetch today. Then get two more estimates to substantiate the first.

If your realistic resale value looks healthy, the next step is to look at the administrative costs and budget …

SARAH SUGGESTS … 'Do your research well to work out your probable resale price and do be realistic. However good a job you intend to do on a property, it is very difficult to break through the 'ceiling price'. Don't rely on a rise in the market. If you are unrealistic now, you may find that your overspeculation costs you your profit later.'

Administrative costs

Buying a property always costs more than the purchase price. Forget to include the following costs in your calculations and you will get a nasty shock:

CHECKLIST

ADDITIONAL COSTS OF BUYING PROPERTY
- ☐ Legal fees – solicitor/conveyancer's fees, which start at about £400
- ☐ Stamp duty – a government tax on properties for sale over £60,000
- ☐ Borrowing set-up costs and interest – if you need a mortgage you will have to pay lender's fees. Your lender will want to carry out a valuation (usually around £150) on the property to check their loan is secure. Some lenders also charge an arrangement fee
- ☐ Cost of survey
- ☐ Land registry costs – approximately £80–150
- ☐ Site services – gas, electricity, water and council tax

Don't forget to include any other administrative costs specific to your project – for example the costs of selling one property to buy another, planning and building control fees, and estate agent's and solicitor's fees for the sale of the property once developed.

The budget

One of the biggest mistakes made by first-time developers is to neglect their budget. Some forget that property developing is a business, others fail to include all of their outgoings in their costings (sometimes simply to kid themselves and make themselves feel better), and most go over budget along the way.

Remember, cash flow is key. No one wants to run short of funds to complete a project or find they have to cut corners to finish a development. Plan your budget rigorously and, just as importantly, stick to it. Work out the budget for the project *before* you buy a property in order to find out whether you are considering a sound investment rather than taking on more than you can handle. The big question is 'how much will all of the work cost?' The maths may seem overwhelming, but you can work out a realistic allocation of costs if you include everything from major repairs to light switches and labour in your calculations. Use the charts on pages 59–63 to make a list of work that needs doing on the property, and approach builders and get quotes for all the necessary work.

If you are not adept at setting budgets, it is easy to overlook key areas, forget to include major works and discover unexpected expenses.

SEE ALSO

Calling in the experts   p 112

CASE STUDY · Maidstone: Focusing on the budget

Window dressers Liz and Laura bought a two-bedroom, terraced house in Maidstone at auction by remortgaging their own homes.

PROJECT COSTS

Cost of property	£90,000	
Renovation budget	£5,000	
Legal fees	£3,000	
Target resale price	£110,000	(similar houses in the area sell for £100,000)
Anticipated pre-tax profit	**£12,000**	

the plan

Liz and Laura could not afford to give up work to concentrate on the project, so they planned to do all of the work on the house in their spare time. They gave themselves a twelve-week deadline. Within this time frame they planned to decorate the two bedrooms, rip out the bathroom and install a new suite, landscape the garden, transform the reception rooms into comfortable living areas and reorganise the kitchen to make it feel more spacious. They also wanted to get rid of the polystyrene tiles on the ceiling of one reception room as well as an old-fashioned fireplace that was not in keeping with their design.

This is how they broke down their budget for the work:

RENOVATION COSTS

Kitchen	£2,100
Bathroom and garden	£700
Decoration	£1,200
Building	£1,000
Contingencies	nil
Total renovation cost	**£5,000**

sarah's advice

My initial impression of Liz and Laura's budget was that it was incredibly tight, with no contingency fund. A contingency fund is crucial to your budget. It's the small amount of emergency money you can draw on when things go wrong, and they often do! For example, you may uncover a problem that needs urgent repair or you may need to enlist extra labour when the going gets tough. The possibilities are incalculable and you need protection against the worst-case scenario.

My second concern was that Liz and Laura had not set themselves a realistic budget. They had no building experience between them and had neglected to have a thorough survey carried out on the property before purchasing it. A survey would have shown them whether the house had any major problems or needed expensive structural repair, which could then be reflected in their budget.

Although Liz and Laura dressed their cellar very nicely, this conversion was not a good solution. The treatment they gave this room meant that the space was even more cramped than before, as well as damp.

Liz and Laura managed to save money by fitting their kitchen themselves.

TIP

Consider a contingency fund as an essential part of your costings, rather than an optional luxury. You should set it at 10% of your overall budget. Omitting a contingency fund is false economy – you may start the project with a little loose change in your pocket, but unexpected turns could leave you with a financial headache.

SEE ALSO

Complying with building regulations   p 116

In addition, Liz and Laura had grand ideas for converting the cellar into a habitable room, for which they had not budgeted. An essential part of budgeting is to invest only in projects where you will see a return in your sale price. Your first priority is to make the house fundamentally safe and sound (fixing major problems that arise in a survey); the second is to develop the property in a way that appeals to your target market. The third is to make the finished property attractive to prospective buyers (see Chapter Five). If you are unsure whether 'improvements' will add value, get a second opinion.

I was doubtful that the cellar conversion would be a profitable project in this type of property, but I had to convince our developers. Liz and Laura were told by three different estate agents that money spent on a cellar conversion would not be recuperated in a sale. I felt that the house was already balanced – the layout of two bedrooms and two reception rooms is ideal – and that to rid the cellar of damp and increase a sense of space and light would be unnecessarily expensive and labour intensive. However, Liz and Laura were hooked on the idea. They had estimated a mere £850 from their builder to carry out the work and, despite their overall building budget being only £1,000, were undeterred. They were convinced that the basement would be the space that would see great results from their efforts.

how the project progressed

Instead of digging out the floor to make it damp-proof and create more head height in the cellar, Liz and Laura's builder laid a PVC damp-proof course and screed on top to make it level. The damp walls were left untreated and simply painted. The cellar was left feeling even more cramped and Liz and Laura ran the risk of the damp showing up in a prospective buyer's survey, which could jeopardise a sale. Furthermore, the builder put in a window costing £80, which brought much-needed light and ventilation into the cellar but did not comply with building regulations as it didn't open far enough to be classed as a fire escape. Although Liz and Laura went on to decorate the cellar very nicely, this makeover was not a good solution. The big lesson here is to do a job properly or not at all. Liz and Laura should have spent the £1,000 allowed for

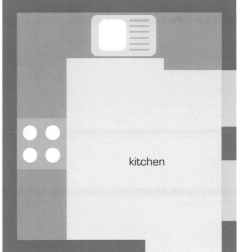

kitchen

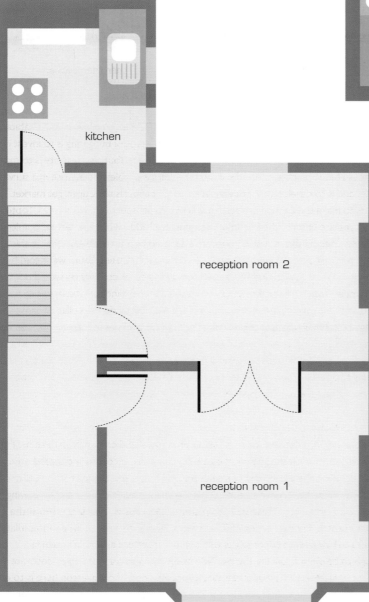

kitchen

reception room 2

reception room 1

Liz and Laura wanted to reorganise the kitchen in their property to make it feel more spacious. A kitchen is a key room, which really helps to sell a house so I welcomed the idea. The best way to maximise space in this room was to block up the cellar door and move it to reception room 2. Slimline units will help make a small kitchen feel more roomy and provide adequate storage. Look for a range that incorporates concealed units and a mini-sized dishwasher if you are trying to squeeze maximum space from a small kitchen.

Liz and Laura made vast improvements to their reception rooms. I would recommend you stage a room to suggest how it can be used with just a few key pieces. Borrowing items from friends and family could save you money.

building costs more efficiently on the property, or saved it as a contingency fund, where it would have been used up amazingly quickly.

Unfortunately, the job of replacing the ceiling in the living room and skimming over the Artex throughout the house came in at an unexpected £600. As the £5,000 total renovation budget faded into the distance Liz and Laura needed to get a grip on that building work!

Fortunately, they did manage to save money by installing the kitchen themselves and incorporating the original enamel bath into their new scheme. They also saved a vast amount on labour by enlisting family and friends to landscape the garden, supply materials and do the plumbing. The extra pairs of hands meant they stayed on schedule, but I would never advocate you risking friendship in business. It also gives you a false budget, as you will see in the final costings opposite.

One of the main reasons that Liz and Laura's budget rocketed was that the pair indulged their passion for window dressing and design. The two dark and dingy reception rooms were successfully transformed into light, modern spaces by replacing the 1960s fireplace and using modern furniture to suggest how the rooms could be used. However, they opted for a feminine scheme of lilac walls and a fleur-de-lis motif, which may not have been to every buyer's taste. You should not be tempted to spend money on personalising a property. Use your budget instead to create a neutral look that will appeal to the widest possible audience.

Staging a house for sale is a good idea but you need only a few pieces of furniture to suggest how a buyer can live in the property. Liz and Laura spent £1,500 on furniture to prop their finished house, regarding the pieces as investments to be utilised in future projects. The cost of the furniture should still be added to the budget for this property, whether it is used again or not. If Liz and Laura's next development was to be of a different scale or style the furniture may not fit and they would have to pay for it to be stored. I would suggest first-time developers borrow furniture from their own house for propping rather than spending money on new items.

SEE ALSO

Sell the lifestyle   p 141

the outcome

Where most developers would consider a property finished, Liz and Laura continued to dress the property. Property developing is all about budget. You need money for furniture and decoration, but you need to know when to stop. Liz and Laura ended up spending £1,900 on staging the property, a big chunk of their anticipated £5,000 budget. Here's how their final sums compared with their original budget:

SUMMARY OF RENOVATION COSTS

	ORIGINAL BUDGET	FINAL SUMS	
Kitchen	£2,100	£1,310	(they installed the kitchen themselves)
Bathroom and garden	£700	£450	(they used friends and family to do the work)
Decorating	£1,200	£1,350	
Building	£1,000	£3,090	(three times the original estimate)
Staging	nil	£1,900	(nothing in the original budget for staging)
Fees and mortgage repayments		£4,200	
Total renovation cost	**£5,000**	**£12,300**	

The final figure for the total renovation cost does not include free labour and materials, which would have cost another £2,500. Remember, if you go over budget, you are depleting your profit. If Liz and Laura were to sell at the ceiling price of £110,000 they would be left with just £7,700 profit before tax.

Lessons learned

Successful property developing requires spending as little as possible for maximum result. The way to do this is to think like a developer. A summary of the above case study will get you in the mindset:

1 **Get a survey done.** Before you purchase any property, make sure you understand its problem, know what work is needed and whether this is the project for you.

2 **Get a second opinion.** Ask an estate agent what will add value to the property. Consider their advice – you are not renovating for yourself.

3 **Adhere to building regulations.** Seek advice from the Building Regulations Officer at your local council planning department. It is illegal not to secure the correct building regulations approval for works done; not doing so can also impact on the survey or the ability of a potential buyer to secure a mortgage on the property.

4 **Do a job properly or not at all.** Doing a job badly is not money well spent.

5 **Decorate for your market, not for yourself.** Don't be tempted to make the space feel too personal.

6 **Don't blow the budget on staging the property.** It is necessary only to suggest how the space could be used.

SEE ALSO	
p 26	The survey
p 116	Complying with building regulations
p 141	Sell the lifestyle

Calculating your renovation budget

All of these pointers will keep you focused on your budget and help you stick to it. Until you have a few projects under your belt, however, it is still easy to miss out details that could cost you in the long run. To make life easier, photocopy the checklists on the following pages and take them with you to viewings. Tick the boxes and pencil in the relevant solution as you view the property. When you are at home you can add in details about the work that needs to be done and work out costings using quotes for each job. This way, you won't forget a thing!

The completed charts will help you calculate your renovation budget. Add this sum to the administrative and purchase costs of the property and subtract this figure from the potential sale price:

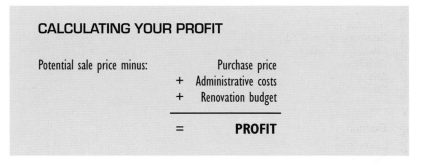

CALCULATING YOUR PROFIT

Potential sale price minus:		Purchase price
	+	Administrative costs
	+	Renovation budget
	=	**PROFIT**

CHAPTER SUMMARY

1 Always be realistic about what you can take on.
2 Make sure it is a deal *before* you commit to a property. Calculate whether the potential sale price less the sum of the purchase price, administrative costs and budget give you a profit margin of 20%. If the sums don't add up, walk away. A better deal could be just around the corner.
3 Decorate for your market – avoid stamping your personality on the space and make only those improvements necessary for your development.
4 If you can't do a job properly don't do it at all. Take responsibility for producing solid, structurally sound work that complies with building regulations and is professionally finished.
5 Always work out a realistic budget and do all you can to stick to it – to lose track of your budget is to lose sight of your profit.
6 Always build a 10% contingency fee into your budget as an essential part of your costings.
7 Appeal to the widest possible market without losing sight of your target market.
8 Know your market and their needs and renovate accordingly.

✓ WORKS CHECKLIST

EXTERNAL RENOVATIONS

	PROBLEM	SOLUTION	COST
External works			
Roof repairs			
Chimney removal, repair, alteration			
Painting			
Windows			
Guttering			
Repointing or rendering			
Extensions or building works			
Demolition			
Skip hire			
Other			
Garden			
Landscaping			
New lawn, patio or decking and paving			
Shrubs, plants, trees			
Fencing			
Shed			
Other			
Entrance			
Front door			
Doorway			
Porch			
Flooring			
Paintwork			
Staircase			
Other			
Tools and equipment			
Hire			
Purchase			
Labour costs including VAT			
Including works overleaf			

WORKS CHECKLIST

INTERNAL RENOVATIONS, ROOM BY ROOM

	FLOORING (E.G. CONCRETE, WOOD, CARPETING)	WALLS AND CEILINGS (E.G. PLASTERING, HACKING OFF, REPLASTERING)	DECORATION (E.G. WALLS, CEILING, WOODWORK)
Bedroom 1			
Bedroom 2			
Bedroom 3			
Bedroom 4			
Bathroom 1			
Bathroom 2			
Study			
Loo			
Utility room			
Kitchen			
Dining room			
Reception room 1			
Reception room 2			
Hallways and landing			
Contingency fund – 10%			
Total cost			

TILING
(E.G. SPLASHBACKS, FLOORING)

WINDOWS
(E.G. REPLACE, FIT DOUBLE-GLAZED UNITS, INSERT VELUX OR NEW FRAMES)

ELECTRICS
(E.G. FITTINGS, LIGHT SWITCHES, SOCKETS, PHONE POINTS)

PLUMBING
(E.G. RADIATORS, BOILER, BATHROOM, KITCHEN)

	JOINERY (E.G. DOORS, BOXING, SKIRTING, CUPBOARDS, SHELVING)	DRESSING (E.G. SOFT FURNISHINGS, FURNITURE, ACCESSORIES)	BATHROOM SUITE (E.G. TAPS)
Bedroom 1			
Bedroom 2			
Bedroom 3			
Bedroom 4			
Bathroom 1			
Bathroom 2			
Study			
Loo			
Utility room			
Kitchen			
Dining room			
Reception room 1			
Reception room 2			
Hallways and landing			
Contingency fund – 10%			
Total cost			

NEW KITCHEN
(E.G. WORKSURFACES,
SINK, TAPS)

WHITE GOODS
(E.G. COOKER, WASHING
MACHINE, DISHWASHER,
FRIDGE FREEZER,
MICROWAVE)

GENERAL STRUCTURAL WORKS
DEMOLITION OF INTERNAL WALLS
INSTALLATION OF NEW INTERNAL WALLS
BUILDING (E.G. CONSERVATORY)
NEW FLOORS LAID THROUGHOUT

BUYING TO LET

What is 'buying to let'?

Many people choose to buy a property, develop it and then let it out rather than sell it.

Their hope is that their capital asset will rise while they receive a stable income through the rental market over a number of years. Obviously, their success relies heavily on the state of the rental marketplace.

The recent explosion in 'Buy to Let'

Throughout the second half of the 1990s, residential property investment became increasingly popular as property prices soared, interest rates dropped and specialist 'buy to let' mortgages were created. These offered preferential rates to individual investors compared with the commercial investment mortgages already available. At the same time the stock market became lacklustre and other forms of long-term investment failed to recover from the unscrupulous salesmen scandals of the late 1980s.

The trend for 'buying to let' continued to increase rapidly, with one survey boasting that lenders advanced a total of 'buy to let' loans worth £6.6 million in 2001 compared with £3 million in 1999. This in itself helped fuel the increase in property prices by an average of 15% in 2001, while the stock market fell by more than 15% in the same period. Many sectors of the general public lost confidence in investing in stocks and shares and, with no other obvious place to invest, even more people were compelled to 'buy to let'.

The market today

There are currently two big questions. Firstly, is there still the high demand for rental properties to match what some describe as a saturated market? Secondly, in the current climate, are 'buy to lets' performing as well as other forms of investment?

At the time of writing, there is still a growth in the rental sector because:

1 **There is a level of apprehension in the property market.** Some would-be buyers are erring on the side of caution and choosing to rent rather than buy or sell, while they wait for both the UK's economic situation and the property market to stabilise.
2 **Would-be first-time buyers are finding it difficult to get on the property ladder.** They are waiting until they are older before buying property – aged 32 in Greater London, the Midlands and the North-East, and 34 in Scotland according to the Halifax. Many young people cannot afford to put down a deposit on a home or afford mortgage repayments on their wage. Despite this, many choose to move out of their family home by their mid-twenties and renting is their most affordable option.
3 **There have been changes to our working practices in recent years.** The increasing number of company relocations – especially from the South-East to East Anglia, the Midlands and the South-West, according to the Halifax – is creating new demand for rental properties. In addition, there are more and more people working on short-term contracts and medium-term placements for several months at a time, as well as workers on contract from overseas.

In short, the rental market in general is still relatively strong. In the first half of 2003, the RICS (Royal Institute of Chartered Surveyors) found that rents in Britain had risen for the first time in two years. However, there are great swathes of the UK where an excess of housing stock to let is driving rents downwards – most notably in major cities and at the cheaper end of the market.

In most areas across the UK, rents have not risen in line with house prices. Despite the recent surge in house prices, neither rental nor sale prices are expected to experience a sharp rise in the near future. Look closely at all other investment options available to you before you choose to invest in a 'buy to let'. It is far from being a guaranteed money-spinner.

Property as pension or investment

It would seem that the days of making fast cash from 'buying to let' are over.

The general consensus among experts is that if you want to make money, you will have to hang on to your rental property for at least ten years. Even then, after all the hard work and stress of renting a property there is still no guarantee that your asset will appreciate in value.

I would still always advise you to look into the state of the market and at predicted conditions even if you are considering a 'buy to let' as a long-term investment. For instance, although interest rates have a direct impact on property prices, it would be unwise to assume that the property market is stable at the moment just because interest rates are currently at a 30-year low.

I would also advise that you look into other forms of investing your hard-earned savings for the future and see how 'buying to let' compares. Remember, too, that capital gains tax means that when you finally decide to sell your 'buy to let', you will in effect be paying 40% of your profit to the tax man.

Consider the following points:

- Pension funds have the benefit of tax relief and are free of capital gains tax.
- You have 100% control over your own funds in a property, but it is a high-risk investment. The Government requires you to put 75% of your pension into an annuity, which needs to be bought by the age of 75.
- Look at the returns from pension plans, for instance by using the index published by Micropal. Compare figures over different time frames so as to take into consideration slumps and rises in the property market and pension funds.

ANOTHER EXPERT'S WORDS ...

According to one sales director: '"Buying to let" makes sense as long as you're not in it for the very short term. If you're buying and you hope to let it for a year and then sell it and make a profit in this market you're not going to do that. But if you're looking at five, ten, fifteen years for school fees, pensions or whatever, it's a definite opportunity.'

SEE ALSO

p 154   Resources

'Property *can* be a great way to plan for a financially secure future based on historical evidence. But before you take the plunge you should research the market, be realistic about the potential rental income you will make from the property and use the tips from this book to ensure you buy well.'

CASE STUDY

Scunthorpe: A 'buy to let' investment

Clergyman Les Whitefield and his wife Judy sank their life savings into a huge derelict house in a remote village in North Lincolnshire. They planned to renovate it, rent it out and have it not only as an investment but also as a home into which they could eventually move when Les retired. They calculated that they could generate an income from the rental over seven or eight years, which would pay for the renovations and possibly contribute towards a lump sum for their retirement. Their calculations were based on the following sums:

PROJECT COSTS/INVESTMENT

Cost of property	£48,000
Renovation budget (including 10% contingency)	£44,000
Target resale value	£105,000
Anticipated profit on resale value	**£13,000**
Plan to rent it out for £600 per month; rental profit over seven years =	**£50,000**

When most people retire, they downsize. Les and Judy fell in love with the property and felt that a larger house would ultimately be worth more as a pension. They had the right idea, but the property market isn't necessarily stable and you need to make sure you buy well.

The most important factor for a 'buy to let' property is its location. Les and Judy had fallen in love with this village just outside Scunthorpe, but would anyone else? A property of this size should appeal to an executive rental market as a family home, but a family would also require good facilities, amenities and transport links. In fact this village has one pub that opens only at lunchtimes, a scanty bus service and no post office or shops. In hard times it may not be easy to rent such a house. You are always better off developing smaller properties in more amenable locations if the rental market in your area is not already flooded with this type of property.

Judy and Les converted their attic to get more out of their property.

the plan

The house itself was vast and needed a great deal of work. In addition, the three-storey property had a derelict stable block, also three storeys high, attached to the end of the house. Les and Judy wanted to knock through to the stable on each level and integrate the extra space into the property. This would add a dining room on the ground floor, another en-suite bedroom on the first floor and extend the loft bedroom at the top of the house.

sarah's advice

I had two worries with their plan. The first was that the house was already enormous for two people and could become unmanageable in their retirement if they went ahead with an extension. Secondly, as a 'buy to let', Les and Judy would make more money and spread the risk of vacancy periods if they kept the stable block separate and turned it into a small, one-bedroom cottage. This would add value to the entire property and provide higher rental returns as well as flexibility.

In the short term, renting out both the cottage and the house would be more profitable than renting out a larger house with one extra bedroom. In my experience, two incomes not only provide more profit than one but, more importantly, also spread any risk. This plan would also give Les and Judy the option of continuing to rent out the cottage when they moved into the house, or vice versa, if they did find the house too roomy in their retirement.

how the project progressed

Les and Judy did some research but decided against the cottage conversion. The planning permission they would require would probably be granted although it would take a while. The planners also envisioned problems integrating a staircase into the building.

For the more inexperienced among us, it is always wise to seek an architect's advice on more complicated design issues such as a staircase. Get one to draw up

SEE ALSO

p 113   Employing
        an architect

p 115   How to apply for
        planning permission

Judy and Les replaced the original picture window. The new addition served a similar function to the original, but had less of the grandeur. They could have saved money and preserved a rare and marketable feature had they chosen to restore it.

plans and submit an application to your local planning department, then sit back and wait for a decision. Incorporating an extra unit within your home is a great way to spread any risk and create a greater income – it can certainly be worth the effort.

Even though Les and Judy began their development as a business venture, they became very attached to their house. Halfway through the project, they seriously considered marketing the property as a holiday let rather than for longer, twelve-month lets, so that they would be able to stay there with their family from time to time. I advised very strongly against this for three reasons:

1 Although the revenue generated by short-term holiday lets is greater on a weekly basis, the revenue generated by a long-term lease is more likely to be higher overall because of vacant periods in holiday lettings.

2 The property was *not* in a holiday location. I did some research and found only one other holiday let nearby, and that stood empty for the majority of the year.

Les and Judy's impressive hallway had all the charm of a period property and all of the appeal of a newly decorated space.

Judy and Les chose to decorate the attic space simply and neutrally. A perfect blank canvass for potential buyers.

3 Finally, if the house was let on a weekend or weekly basis, Judy and Les would need to spend a good deal of time and energy cleaning and preparing the property after every let, and also marketing the property in a constant search for tenants.

Judy and Les's emotions were clouding their business decisions and putting their future financial security on the line. Luckily, they finally saw sense and reverted to their plan for a long-term lease.

the outcome

When Les and Judy finally finished all of renovation work, we called in the agents to value the property for rental. They speculated that the Whitefields could charge up to £800 per calendar month in rent. Because Les and Judy's budget had dramatically escalated throughout the project, however, their return on investment was lower, meaning any lump sum after costs at retirement would be considerably less.

I saw another option – a sale. The property market had been rising during their refurbishment and this, together with the renovation work they had done, resulted in the house having almost quadrupled in value. Les and Judy had taken a big risk in buying this property, but it appeared to have paid off (see figures overleaf). What started out as a dream ended up as a financial investment. By renting it out, they would not only have to manage the property, but have to rely on it being rented out, putting all their eggs into one basket, which is risky. You cannot bank on the rental market holding for a long period of time.

Estate agents recommended an asking price of up to £195,000 for the renovated property. If they decided to sell rather than to let, Les and Judy would make more money for their retirement and could release their profit to buy two smaller projects to rent out, spreading the rental risk. It is far easier to let smaller properties and Les and Judy would have the option of living in one property while renting out the other for a regular income – a realistic option considering that on retirement they wouldn't need such a large house.

SUMMARY OF PROJECT COSTS

	ORIGINAL BUDGET	FINAL SUMS
Cost of property	£48,000	£48,000
Renovation budget (including 10% contingency)	£44,000	£70,000
Total investment	£92,000	£118,000
Target resale value	£105,000	£190,000
Projected profit	**£13,000**	**£72,000**
	(excluding rise in market)	**(including rise in market)**

Les and Judy's new kitchen was impressive, although I wondered if their market would be looking for a large table for family meals, rather than a breakfast bar.

SARAH SUGGESTS ... 'If you are planning on investing in property for financial security in your retirement, never take more risks than you have to.'

Financing a 'buy to let'

Another factor fuelling the boom in the 'buy to let' market is the advent of specially tailored mortgages.

Until relatively recently, buying a property to produce an income was viewed as a commercial undertaking. Borrowers were required to pay commercial rates of interest and their income was less important when assessing their ability to repay their mortgage.

Things have now changed. Lack of choice between renting and buying is seen as bad for the economy and many lenders consider that the private rental sector should be encouraged. 'Buy to let' mortgages recognise that rental income will be used to service the loan and they offer non-commercial rates. This is all good news if 'buying to let' is for you. It is worth shopping around to find the right deal, be it interest-only, repayment, endowment or PEP-linked loans, but the general characteristics are as follows:

- 'Buy to let' mortgages are generally available for between five and 45 years and for up to 80% of the property's value.
- Your rental income can be taken into account and you will be able to make taxable deductions against the rental income for costs such as insurance, maintenance fees, agent's fees and other expenses.
- You can claim for replacing items of furniture, fittings or fixtures although their original costs are not tax deductable. Alternatively, you may find a 'wear and tear' allowance based on 10% of your rental income is deductible.
- Insurance cover is available for the buildings and contents insurance, as well as legal expenses in the event of court action against a defaulting tenant.
- It is now possible to invest in a 'buy to let' mortgage for multiple property investments as well as a first or second mortgage.
- Many lenders expect landlords to use a letting agent to manage the property and for a contract or Assured Shorthold Tenancy Agreement (see page 92) to be drawn up.

Additional costs

To make financial sense your gross rents should generally be at least between 130 and 150% of your monthly mortgage repayment. This helps budget for the additional financial commitments required when 'buying to let', which many investors underestimate.

All of the following seemingly little extras can add to your capital outlay and reduce your net income, even when you can deduct costs for 'wear and tear':

1 **Maintenance fees.** These include the cost of cleaning communal areas, general repairs to the property, replacing damaged furniture and redecorating rooms regularly.

2 **Vacant periods.** You may experience vacant periods or have to take a cut in the rental price due to market conditions. Annual rental yields can be as much as 8–9% of the value of the property nationwide and up to 10% in London but remember that this is a gross figure, which is accurate only if your property is let 365 days a year. You need

SEE ALSO

p 22   Funding your purchase

to set aside money to cover your mortgage for several months should there be a break between lets.

3 Falling rents. Remember, rents can fall as well as rise. The reality is that an overpriced house may sell, but an overpriced house for rent almost certainly will not.

4 Buildings insurance. This is calculated on the cost of rebuilding. The larger the property, the higher it is likely to be.

5 Agents' fees. If you to choose to pay for help with the management of your property and in finding tenants, then you will also have to include agents' fees in your calculations. These vary between 8 and 15% of your rental income.

6 Tax. Remember, your rental income is just that, an income. As such, you will need to pay tax on it. While you can offset the cost of actually running your 'buy to let', your mortgage repayments must be paid net of tax. For further advice I would strongly suggest you contact an accountant or financial advisor as everyone's personal tax situation is different.

For a realistic calculation of your profit, deduct all of these additional costs from your rental income to work out how much you are likely to make. The good news is that the tenant is generally responsible for council tax, any utility bills and a TV licence.

Remember that you will then need to deduct an appropriate amount of tax depending on the tax band you are in. If this final figure leaves you struggling to meet mortgage repayments, then proceed with caution or at your peril!

CALCULATING YOUR RENTAL PROFIT

Rental income minus:

$$\begin{array}{r} \text{Maintenance fees} \\ + \quad \text{4 months without a tenant} \\ + \quad \text{Insurance} \\ + \quad \text{Agents' fees/cost of your own labour} \\ \hline = \quad \textbf{REALISTIC GROSS PROFIT} \end{array}$$

SEE ALSO

Managing a 'buy to let'   p 90

SARAH SUGGESTS ... 'If the rental you receive from your property is around 130% of your mortgage repayments then letting may be a financially viable option for you.'

Top ten tips for 'buying to let'

If 'buying to let' stacks up as a good investment for you personally, then there are some things to bear in mind before you start looking for the perfect property.

Careful planning is key:

1 Do your research. Check local rental conditions, analyse rental demand and determine the types of tenant renting in your area. Look for obvious clues such as a large company relocation, the opening of trendy bars and shops (attractive to young professionals) or the existence of good schools nearby (attractive to families), and choose a property with features that will appeal to your market.

2 Ideally, your rental property should be close to transport links and/or has off-street parking.

3 If you intend to rent your property to professionals, every bedroom should ideally be a double (even if it is a small double).

4 Think low maintenance. You want a property that will run itself as smoothly as possible.

5 If you are managing the property yourself, be prepared to do some hard work. A 'buy to let' property is far from being a hassle-free income.

6 Choose a property close to home, which will enable you to pop over and sort out any problems easily. If you are not able to do this it can cost you more than a week's rent to get someone in.

7 Remember that family rental homes require plenty of space and storage.

8 If you are the sole freeholder of the property, you will need to ensure that the common parts and the exterior of the property are well maintained. You may wish to spend a couple of hours a week vacuuming and polishing or employ a professional cleaning company to keep these areas up to scratch. If your 'buy to let' is leasehold, however, the responsibility for the maintenance of the exterior and interior communal areas will rest with the freeholder unless your lease specifies otherwise.

9 Avoid large gardens, especially in a town property, unless you intend adding the cost of a gardener to the weekly rental and you are aiming to market your property as a family home. As any keen gardener knows, it doesn't take long for a little neglect to start to really show.

10 Should you let furnished or unfurnished? Sometimes there is little difference between the rents commanded by unfurnished compared with part- or fully furnished properties to let. It all depends on your market and the demand in your area. Before you go looking for furniture, do your research and find the best option for you. (If you choose furnished, see Chapter Five for some advice on design and decoration.)

SEE ALSO

p 38   Identifying your target market

p 90   Managing a 'buy to let'

p 124 Maximising the appeal of your 'buy to let'

Why 'let to buy' is the new 'buy to let'

If you like the financial returns offered by 'buying to let', but want to move home yourself, you should consider 'letting to buy'.

The house price crash of the early 1990s was the birth of 'letting to buy'. Many home owners in negative equity found that they were unable to sell their properties for the amount they had paid for them. Rents were high and home owners found that their mortgage payments didn't stretch far enough to fund buying a second home. Many decided to let their homes and buy a much smaller property to reduce their outgoings.

SARAH SUGGESTS … 'If neither "buying to let" nor "letting to buy" seem a viable option for you, you can always consider renting out a room in your own home to accrue extra income from your property. This is especially useful and least stressful if you rent for a relatively short period so as to fund your next property purchase.'

The situation today

In the current economic climate, 'letting to buy' is a choice rather than a necessity. Rather than selling a home to fund a new purchase, some home owners are taking advantage of the low interest rates and are, in theory, improving their pension prospects by renting out a property they no longer want to live in, in order to cover a second mortgage. Others are choosing to rent out a property rather than sell it due to the perceived instability of the property market.

It now takes typically sixteen weeks to sell a London property, compared with twelve weeks in 2002. This, coupled with price falls of up to 20% for higher priced properties in the capital, is causing concern. Similarly, the Home Sale Network, a group of 720 independent agents specialising in mid- and lower-priced homes, reports that in the summer of 2003 property across England and Wales was taking an average of six weeks to find a buyer – a week longer than in March 2003 – and average sale prices have fallen from 97% of asking prices in the spring to a current 95.6%.

Much of the reason for this is that the amount people perceive their home to be worth and the actual value of their property are often two very different figures. When there was a shortage of property on the market a few years ago vendors could be greedy, but those days are past. If you really want to sell you have to be realistic about the asking price.

'Letting to buy' sounds like a good prospect in today's climate, but think hard before you rush into anything.

TIPS ON LETTING TO BUY

- Do your research. Check with a letting agent that your home is 'lettable'. Small houses and flats situated near town centres, business parks, colleges or a university and near to travel links are often good.

- To make 'letting to buy' viable, experts recommend that the rent you receive from your property should be around 130% of your mortgage repayments.

- Consider mortgaging to free equity for a deposit on your next home, but be cautious not to stretch yourself too far financially or you may end up regretting it.

- The rental market is competitive. Ensure your property is well designed and furnished in a style appropriate for your target rental market. It may once have been your home, but look at it objectively and make any appropriate alterations (see Chapter Five for ideas and inspiration).

- If you let the property for any length of time and it is not your main residence, remember that any increase in value may be taxable when you sell – check with your local tax office.

- Keep up to date with tax rules as they change annually.

PROPERTY POINTER ...

'"Letting to buy" works best with an average or below-average priced property. You may struggle to get enough rent to pay a mortgage on an expensive home.'

CHAPTER SUMMARY

1 Research the market extensively before you 'buy to let'. Find out what is happening in the rental market, be realistic about what you can take on and the profit you will receive *before* you invest.

2 Make sure it is a deal. Your realistic gross profit will derive from the rental income less maintenance fees, perhaps four months without a tenant, insurance, agents' fees or the cost of your own labour.

3 Letting may be financially viable if the rental you receive from the property is around 130% of your mortgage repayments.

4 Be prepared for some hard work if you manage the property yourself.

5 A rental property without good transport links and/or off-street parking is hard to let to most markets.

6 Tailor your 'buy to let' property to your market.

7 Go for a low-maintenance 'buy to let' property so as to minimise day-to-day hassle.

MANAGING PROPERTY

Managing a development
Managing a 'buy to let'

Managing a development

A successful development is partly dependent on a smooth running site. Whether you choose to develop one property at a time, or several, you will need to do some careful planning to ensure that your site(s) stay on schedule.

The first decision you should make is whether to oversee the development yourself or to employ an experienced project manager.

Project managing

Project managing is one of the most important roles on-site. The responsibilities of a project manager include:

1 Running the site from the beginning to the end of the project.
2 Ensuring that the site complies with building regulations and permissions.
3 Ensuring the site is safe.
4 Hiring all the contractors and tradesmen needed for the job.
5 Scheduling their works in sequential order and making sure this work is carried out within the budget and time-scale agreed with the owner of the property.
6 Paying the contractors' wages and complying with current subcontractor tax regulations.
7 Ordering all the materials required.
8 Arranging for the right supplies to arrive at the right time.
9 Making big decisions, but also clearing up the site and ensuring there is tea, coffee and loos available.
10 Usually being on-site approximately six days a week for at least several hours, arriving around 7.00 a.m. The project manager is inevitably the person putting in the extra labour if things run behind schedule.

In short, you need a lot of time, energy and the right contacts to even think about project managing your own development. You also need to have the personality to run the site like a military operation, as well as developing a good working relationship with everyone involved with the project. A happy team means you are more likely to accomplish good results and swift work, all of which will get you nearer your profit faster.

Before contemplating whether you can fit into this role, make sure you can afford to do so, in both senses of the word.

can you afford to spend adequate time on-site?

If you are committed to another full-time job, then the answer is most probably 'no'. If your working hours are flexible then you must think of project managing one site as a full-time job, no less. In my experience, you will not be able to work elsewhere for a large chunk of the day and simultaneously fit in working on-site, overseeing labour and ordering materials into 24 hours. Rule number one is to be realistic about what you can take on.

SEE ALSO

Complying with building regulations	p 116
Calling in the experts	p 112

can you afford to give up the day job?

The workload associated with this role means that project managers usually command a payment of at least 10% of the cost of the project. For this reason, many first-time developers think that overseeing their project themselves will save them money. But this is the case only if things run smoothly on-site. Inexperience can result in hiccups, a change of plans partway through a development or overruns in budget and schedule, all of which can have costly consequences. Rule number two is to take a long look at your salary. If you are earning enough to pay a project manager, then question why you shouldn't.

Doing your own project management

There is a lot to be said for handing over the stresses of the day-to-day running of a project to an experienced manager. However, if you feel you are up to the challenge and are committed to doing it yourself, here are some tips to help you get off to a good start:

1 **Get your site organised as soon as contracts are exchanged.** Source your materials now and find the right contractors and tradesmen for the job as soon as the sale is complete.

2 **Have back-up tradesmen and builders on standby.** Ask friends or fellow developers for recommendations. Buy an address book just for your development projects and start to build up good contacts. You never know when you will need them.

3 **Draft a schedule of works that needs to happen on-site and when.** This will allow you to order materials at the right time. Too much arriving too early will result in a cluttered site. Not only will you have a security risk, but you will find that you have to constantly shift heavy items from room to room so tradesmen can do their work. Doing this also increases the risk of the goods being damaged. Too much too late means that jobs come to a standstill and your schedule slides. If you are sourcing materials from overseas check that the shipping time fits with your schedule.

4 **Using your schedule, keep a wall chart** (see pages 82–3) of contractors' and tradesmen's tasks and when you want them to start and finish work. The key to sticking to your schedule and therefore your budget, is making sure that the right people start the right jobs and finish them when you need them too. It's all in the timing.

5 **Be crystal clear with your workmen.** Always work out exactly what you want done before you request a quote for a job, however small. Prepare two copies of the details, including drawings – give one to the contractor and keep one for yourself. Vague or incomplete instructions can produce unexpected results.

6 **Control your contractor's costs.** Always negotiate fees upfront and stick to a written agreement, unless unforeseen circumstances arise and change the work that needs to be done or how it can be carried out.

7 **Keep on top of all the work that happens on-site** so that you can be sure you are happy with the quality of the work. Always pay contractors on time, but also make sure you are happy with the results of their labour before doing so.

8 **Stay on top of your paperwork and keep a constant eye on your budget.**

9 **Be realistic about your capabilities.** If you are new to developing property, don't try to dabble in complicated building processes or difficult features and finishes. Avoid a renovation project that is too big for you to handle.

CASE STUDY

SWANSEA

FULL-TIME DEVELOPING

Jo and Angela each had an income of £50,000 before they quit their jobs to be full-time developers and look for a new way of life. They had some DIY experience and project managed their work themselves in just fourteen weeks.

Their tight budget forced them to do most of the work themselves. Their job was a little rushed and this may have been a factor in their house sticking on the market. Having given up their jobs, Jo and Angela had no alternative source of income. Their savings and capital were tied up in the house and, until a sale was agreed, they could not release capital to pursue their next development. Despite an increase in the price of housing in the area, they had to drop the asking price. The house eventually sold after eight weeks on the market for £54,000, giving them a profit of £12,500 each for their 22-week project.

I admire their courage and their brave decision to follow their dream of developing, but you have to be practical about how much money you can live off. Only be your own project manager, if you can do a great job and build up a good reputation. If not, employ a project manager and skilled contractors and stay at work.

see page 43
for more on their project

CHARTING THE PROGRESS OF YOUR DEVELOPMENT

LOCATION	NAME OF CONTRACTOR	CONTACT DETAILS	ESTIMATED COSTS

DATE WORK COMMISSIONED	DATE WORK EXPECTED TO FINISH	ACTUAL COSTS	WORK STILL TO BE COMPLETED

Managing more than one property

If you have built up some experience developing property and several suitable ventures become available, you may wish to develop more than one property at once.

Doing so may spread your financial risk but will also increase the chances of things going wrong. Here are some tips for keeping things running smoothly when you can't be in several places at once:

- Think carefully before you take on multiple projects. Get some financial advice and make sure that you don't overstretch yourself. Think about what will happen if both sites do not sell/rent.
- Make sure you employ a very capable foreman on each site to keep things running smoothly and the site tidy.
- Keep on top of your paperwork and your budgets. If you don't know what you have spent on which site, you don't know whether it will make a profit.
- Avoid robbing Peter to pay Paul. If one site is running over budget, don't be tempted to steal funds from another.
- There are some positive implications of running more than one site simultaneously. Consider bulk buying, for example. You can negotiate better discounts the more materials you buy at the same time, so get organised.
- Keep a cool head. If you come across a problem, stop and think logically before you act upon it, even when time is key. It is always costly to go back on a decision. Sometimes a brief pause to think can save you thousands of pounds.

SARAH SUGGESTS ... 'It is essential you are realistic about how much profit you need to make a year before you think about developing full-time and giving up the day job. You may like the idea of being your own boss, but it is not an easy option.'

CASE STUDY

Aberdare: Going it alone

Patrick and Vanessa Jeffree remortgaged their own home to buy two cottages in the Welsh mining town of Aberdare. They planned to knock the cottages together into one big house and sell it to make a profit of £15,500. This was the first time either of them had taken on a project like this, but they hoped it would make them a fortune.

Aberdare was a good location for property developers to invest in. The town centre had recently been revamped, there were good transport links to Cardiff and Newport and plenty of countryside in between. House prices had risen by 30% the previous year, while prices around the UK had generally dipped. The couple hoped that by creating a four-bedroom house out of two small cottages, they could sell the completed property to a young family for a healthy profit.

They knew, however, that they would have to work hard for their money. The cottages were situated just outside the town centre on a busy road and were in terrible condition. One had been rented out before being placed on the market, the other had been empty for twenty years and was almost derelict.

Despite having little experience, Patrick and Vanessa planned to do most of the work themselves to bring the project in on budget. They set aside £12,500 to renovate the property and, despite their full-time jobs, gave themselves just five weeks to complete this mammoth task.

PROJECT COSTS

Cost of property	£25,000
Renovation budget	£12,500
Target resale price	£53,000
Anticipated pre-tax profit	**£15,500**

the plan

Knocking two properties together meant that Patrick and Vanessa would effectively be creating a new property for just £12,500. This sum had to cover a new central heating system, two new bathrooms, a new kitchen, new windows throughout, complete rewiring of both properties as well as complete replastering, redecoration and newly situated stairs.

Managing a project should start way before work commences on-site, as good planning is crucial. Vanessa and Patrick set their renovation budget by calculating the maximum resale price of the property, minus what they bought it for, rather than on what the work may actually cost. This was a big mistake. Patrick and Vanessa needed to set a realistic budget based on what things would cost or there was a real danger they would be unable to make any money on this development.

The couple also had the added complication of not knowing how much work they were taking on before pricing the job. They bought the cottages at auction,

	SEE ALSO
p 19	Buying at auction
p 58	Calculating your renovation budget

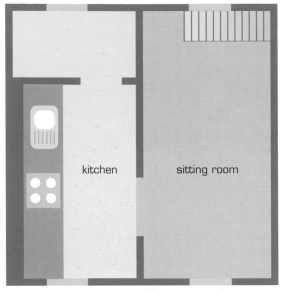

ground floor

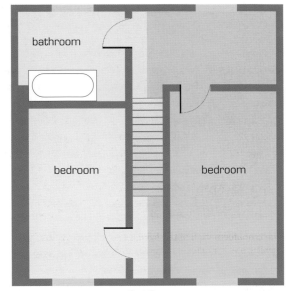

first floor

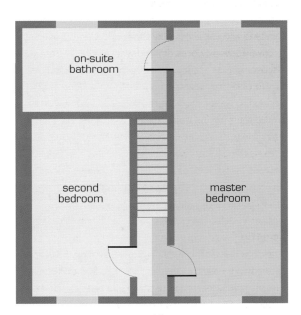

second floor

The original layout of the two tiny cottages meant that the rooms were spread out over three floors, with just one room on each floor. Patrick and Vanessa intended knocking them through to create one larger house with four bedrooms, two bathrooms and a main reception room and kitchen/diner on the ground floor.

■ original cottage
■ attached cottage

SEE ALSO

| Buying at auction | p 19 |
| The survey | p 26 |

without viewing them. Patrick had visited the town previously only on business and didn't realise the site was on a busy road where a car dealer parks all of his cars and two pubs have late licences, which could put off their target market. Always thoroughly check the area and location you are buying or you could just find that your dream home is sat next to a sewage farm! Buying at auction can be a great way to find a bargain, but to do so you need to know what you are doing. It is also crucial that you have a survey carried out on a property you are interested in. I would have

The transformation of the living room in Vanessa and Patrick's cottage is clearly impressive. But a few well chosen pieces of furniture would have gone even further to show viewers how to use this small but beautifully formed space.

recommended a thorough survey for cottages of this age and state of repair. Only then can you anticipate the extent of the work that needs to be taken on, before you invest. Weeks after buying the cottages, Patrick and Vanessa had the cottages surveyed and found out why the properties had been so cheap. The survey uncovered woodworm, dry and wet rot everywhere. Just days into the project, they discovered that treatment for the problem would cost them £1,500 of their budget.

To claw back some of their budget they needed to make cutbacks. Vanessa decided to project manage the scheme, despite working full time, while Patrick drew up the plans for the remodelling of the cottages himself, as well as designing the stairs. He had never done this before, but persisted with his designs and technical drawings. The layout of a property is critical to its success. If you are making major changes, I would always recommend employing an expert to ensure the designs are accurate or you could end up with a house that simply doesn't work. The plans you draw up also need to meet building regulations.

how the project progressed

Patrick perfected his plans and had the staircase made and fitted. It all looked good but he had forgotten to contact the building department. Realising afterwards that the staircase needed to adhere to building regulations, Patrick called for an inspection. The department responded quickly and visited the property the next day. The new staircase did not comply with fire safety regulations. The inspector needed the structure moved which meant that the whole layout of the property would need to change. If the inspector had seen the plans before work had started, the changes could have been made at the planning stage. Although Patrick and Vanessa were desperate to save money, moving the landings, staircase and walls ended up costing them an extra £3,500. Vanessa did manage to save about £1,000 by managing the project herself, but her inexperience meant that she scheduled jobs to happen in the wrong order. They had already rewired the upstairs bedroom and all of the work had to be ripped out.

SEE ALSO

p 80   Managing a development

p 112   Calling in the experts

p 116   Complying with building regulations

Twelve weeks into the project and Vanessa and Patrick had lost control of the job and their budget, which was teetering around £22,000. They now had to get their budget on track and the build under control. They needed to watch every penny and plan work carefully into a time-effective schedule. They could have kept the original kitchen, which was of good quality and condition and suited the style of the house, but Patrick and Vanessa decided against this and sold the original kitchen to fund the purchase of a new one with more units. It was good that they were making money from the kitchen but they were not thinking like developers. They could have easily added a dresser or similar freestanding units to the room, polishing off the look with new worktops, new doors and handles to update the kitchen. It is always crucial to evaluate what you have in a property before you rip it out. I was pleased that Patrick and Vanessa decided to recycle the existing bath and shower.

With no one leading the project while Vanessa and Patrick were working, the project ground to a halt, with only four weeks left in the schedule.

Patrick and Vanessa needed to give the project one final big burst of energy to get the job done. However, just as their spirits were rising, Patrick was made redundant. The couple had remortgaged their own home to finance the cottages and now had only Vanessa's income to pay for the project. In the face of losing everything, they were incredibly determined. Patrick took on project managing the job full time while Vanessa was at work and he was on-site every day. Despite having no DIY experience he got stuck in and learnt on the job. Patrick and Vanessa had to take charge of the budget, as their overspend at this point meant that after four months of hard work they would have only £3,000 to show for their endeavours if they achieved the ceiling price for the property.

BUDGETING TIPS

- Always be realistic about what everything will cost when you put together your budget.
- It is paramount to have a contingency for when things go wrong because they always will, and keep track of everything you spend on the project so that you are able to make cutbacks where necessary.
- Developing on a small budget is always more difficult but not impossible.
- Sourcing your own fittings instead of the builder doing it, means you will get the discount not them.
- Get your kitchen directly from suppliers rather than the retailers, Patrick and Vanessa saved £600 doing this and saved a further £600 by fitting the kitchen themselves.
- Don't be tempted to take on more than you can handle. Don't jeopardise the quality of the job and remember it costs time and money to put mistakes right. To stand a chance of getting top price on this project, Patrick and Vanessa needed to pay attention to their finish.

Vanessa and Patrick could have saved money by working with their existing kitchen. It was good quality and fitted well with the style of the property.

the outcome

Vanessa and Patrick had chosen their builder well and he agreed to stay on the project despite having another job booked. With only a week to go, they finally started work on the garden. With no back garden they needed to make the most of what they had at the front to create a good first impression, deflect attention from the main road and show any interested family that there was some outside space.

Vanessa and Patrick finally completed the project, minutes before the first viewing. The new house was a triumph. What had been two empty falling-down cottages had become one fantastic family home. It was light, airy and modern, while retaining a sense of its history. Downstairs the living room still felt small and was neither defined as a reception room nor dressed, but Vanessa and Patrick felt that prospective buyers would be able to envisage their own furniture there. The kitchen/diner looked impressive. Although they really needed to save the money, they had chosen a sleek modern look and dressed the room with a table to define the eating area.

The new layout worked well. The first and second floors contained three spacious bedrooms and one smaller bedroom. Vanessa and Patrick had put some furniture in the smallest rooms to show how the spaces could be used, although they didn't add much storage. The bathroom had an excellent finish. The jewel in the project, however, was the master bedroom. The cool white room screamed luxury and the en suite took it to another dimension. The decorative finish and attention to detail was excellent throughout and I was really impressed. The garden, however, still needed some TLC. Patrick and Vanessa should have returfed the lawn immediately. Considering the spiralling budget, this would have been money well spent to get viewers through the front door.

With the project now finished and the house looking gorgeous it was time to get those crucial valuations. The final renovation cost of £27,000 meant that Patrick and Vanessa had invested £52,000 in the project. The project had taken three months to complete and earlier estimates suggested the finished product would be worth

For me, the most successful room in Vanessa and Patrick's property was the master bedroom.

£53,000. If they sold for this sum they would make only £1,000. I really hoped that the market had risen and the couple would get more for all of their hard work.

Thankfully, three agents valued the property up to £70,000 under the prevailing market conditions. The couple decided to put the property on the market for between £73,000 and £75,000, and received an offer of £75,950.

Amazing determination and self-belief saw Patrick and Vanessa through their project, but I wouldn't recommend this way of working to anyone.   ✍

SUMMARY OF PROJECT COSTS

	ORIGINAL BUDGET	FINAL SUMS
Cost of property	£25,000	£25,000
Renovation budget (including 10% contingency)	£12,500	£27,000
Total investment	£37,500	£52,000
Target resale value	£53,000	£75,000
Projected profit	**£15,500** (excluding rise in market)	**£23,000** (including rise in market)

Managing a 'buy to let'

To develop property for profit, you need to adopt a myriad of roles and successfully juggle them. If you decide to 'buy to let', you will need to add 'landlord' to your repertoire.

Being a landlord no longer means that you have to find a tenant, organise the legal paperwork, deal with problems and maintain your property all on your own, unless you choose to. There are a number of routes, services and agents available to help you let out your property and manage it. Of course, they all come at a cost.

Depending on your situation, you may choose to go it alone – finding your own tenant and managing all aspects of the property yourself – or to employ a letting agent to provide one of the following four options:

1 **Introduction service.** The agent simply finds you a tenant – approximate commission 10% of the monthly rental income.
2 **Introduction and rent collection.** The agent finds a tenant and administers rent collection each month – approximate commission 12.5% of the monthly rental income.
3 **Full management service.** The agent finds a tenant, administers rent collection and manages the property, including any necessary repairs – approximate commission 15%+ of the monthly rental income.
4 **Full management service, plus rental guarantee.** The agent finds a tenant, administers rent collection and manages the property, including any necessary repairs, plus guarantees a percentage of the rent – approximate commission 17%+ of the monthly rental income.

Finding a good managing agent

Essentially, you should look for an agent who is active and proactive in your local area. If you are going to hand over a percentage of your hard-earned rental income to an agent, you want to have full confidence in their ability to fulfil the services you require.

Visit three local agencies, with a clear idea of the role you wish them to take (see above) and how many of the responsibilities you are happy to look after yourself. Then, ask them the following questions:

1 How do they market the lets in their area? Their answer will give you an indication of the company's profile, as well as the lengths they go to to find tenants.
2 How many potential tenants do they have on their books?
3 Do they belong to any of the national letting agents organisations? Organisations such as ARLA (Association of Residential Letting Agents) or NAEA (National Association of Estate Agents) are able to offer support and guidance should you fall into dispute with one of their member agents. In addition, NAEA requires those of its members involved in lettings to hold 'client money protection cover', which guarantees your money up to a certain limit, should the letting agent go out of business.
4 Do they have professional indemnity insurance?

> **TIP**
> Look on the internet and in letting agents' brochures to see the rental prices commanded by similar properties.

In addition, ask them for a list of their services and fees so you know exactly what you get for your money. Check that the agent is able to provide you with the basics – a signed tenancy agreement, inventory, references, employer's contact details, at least one month's deposit and one month's rent in advance from a future tenant. Lastly, insist that the rent is paid by direct debit, straight into your bank account.

If you decide to hire a letting agent, you will need to organise a valuation. As with selling a property, set up three valuations with different companies.

As advised in the last chapter, your gross rents should be between 130 and 150% of your monthly mortgage repayment to make financial sense. You will now need to assess whether your net rental income covers both your mortgage costs and your management fees and still leaves you with a sufficient profit to make the project worthwhile. Remember that this profit may be called upon to cover costs of vacant periods if the property lies unoccupied at any time.

A landlord's responsibilities

Whether you employ a letting agent or not, there are still some responsibilities which you, as a landlord, will need to undertake by law:

CHECKLIST

LANDLORDS' OBLIGATIONS

☐ You will need a certificate to prove that any gas appliances and gas boilers are safe.

☐ You will need to ensure that there are adequate fire escapes and fire extinguishers and that you meet all fire regulations. Check with your council as different rules govern different types of property.

☐ All soft furnishings and upholstered furniture must comply with fire regulations (see 'Soft Furnishings', page 126) and be made from non-flammable materials.

☐ You will need buildings insurance to cover the property. Take the opportunity to have additional clauses added, which protect the tenant against injury while staying on the premises as well as protecting the property from any malicious damage that occurs under the tenant's care.

☐ I would also recommend you have an electrician service any electrical appliances or plugs. Although this is not currently mandatory, changes are anticipated in the near future. Make sure you know your obligations.

Handling tenants yourself

If you are tempted to go it alone, I would strongly advise you do *all* of the following:

1 Do some serious research into the rent commanded by similar properties in your area. Look at the property press, letting agents' websites on the internet and the local newspapers. Be realistic when deciding on a monthly figure, so that you neither price yourself out of the market nor fall short of the market value.

2 Have an Assured Shorthold Tenancy Agreement drawn up. This a legally binding document designed to protect both the landlord and the tenant. You can buy a ready-made contract or ask your solicitor to draft the agreement for you.

3 If you are letting a part- or fully furnished property, get an impartial expert to draw up a legally binding inventory for you and your tenant. This will give you as landlord the right to hold back part or all of a deposit if any items are damaged during the tenant's stay.

4 Build up a contacts book, via personal recommendations, so that you have reliable tradesmen such as a plumber and electrician on file that you can call upon. Don't wait for a crisis to happen.

5 Encourage your tenants to pay you by standing order. They are easy to set up between banks and will minimise the hassle of having to chase rent.

6 Keep handy a note of tenants' contact details, for example e-mail, work and mobile telephone numbers.

7 Leave a list of useful contact details in the rental property so that tenants can easily contact service providers and the council without calling you first. Remember to include your own details in the list. Your phone number is essential and your tenant should be able to reach you at all times, even when you are abroad, in case of emergency.

8 Leave instructions for operating the central heating, hot water and electric shower, for example, together with any relevant guarantees.

9 Keep at least two spare sets of keys yourself so that you can lend them out to contractors or to tenants if they mislay theirs or lock themselves out. Make sure you retain the master set as keys cut from copies are never as good as the original.

10 Make appointments to inspect the property periodically with your tenant. Get fixed the little jobs that you notice when you visit, such as wobbly door handles, so that they don't escalate, and have boilers serviced regularly so they are less likely to let you down. Remember that your tenant reserves the right to disallow you entry to the property unless you make prior arrangement to visit them and have a verbal confirmation from them that this is convenient.

PROPERTY POINTER ...

'If you manage a property yourself, don't be tempted to let it to people you know. This can complicate the tenant/landlord relationship and contribute to problems, such as late payment of rent.'

SARAH SUGGESTS ... 'Make appointments to inspect the property periodically with your tenant and try to keep on top of repairs, however costly, so that the property does not deteriorate.

Managing more than one 'buy to let'

If you decide to manage more than one 'buy to let' property at once, you will need to be incredibly organised. When there are double or triple chances of things going wrong, there are some ideas to make life easier. My biggest tip would be to adopt a uniform approach to help you be organised, for example:

- Get all your tenants to pay their rent on the same day each month to make checking up on rents and your cash flow easier.
- Try to ensure that gas checks are carried out on the same day every year for all properties. This not only helps you keep up to date but also minimises the cost of employing a plumber (who must be CORGI registered) as you can hire one person to check all the gas appliances on one day rather than on the odd occasion here and there. In addition, having regular checks avoids potential problems with gas appliances.
- Try to stick to the same paint colours in all properties so that touching up in between tenants can be done with just the one pot of paint.
- Buy the same sitting room suites for all properties. As parts wear out you can discard tatty pieces, but still make up a matching set in at least one property.

Other ideas for being organised involve keeping on top of your paperwork with the help of your computer. Use a database or spreadsheets to keep track of tenants' payments so that you know when the rent is due or what you are owed. Set up a separate spreadsheet with dates of your tenants' leases.

Another tip is to create systems for your keys using colours or numbers. Keep them clearly labelled to avoid getting them muddled up.

Lastly, spread your risk. It's best not to have several properties in one apartment block, for example, so that you can increase your chances of having all your properties let at once.

DIY or call in the professionals?

Now you are armed with information about 'buy to let', you need to decide whether to self-manage, or call in the experts. Use the charts opposite and overleaf to help you weigh up all the pros and cons.

'Don't forget, the more properties you own that are let, the more hassle you will have for your money. Think carefully about whether this is really something you want to do and if you are actually motivated enough to make this type of business venture happen.'

SELF-MANAGING A RENTAL PROPERTY

PROS	CONS
• You will receive all of the rental income minus any costs and your mortgage repayments, rather than handing over 10–17% to a letting agent.	• Marketing your property can be costly and you will need to pay to advertise up-front, before receiving a rental income.
• You will have more control over who rents your property. You can hand pick your tenants and when you meet possible tenants you can use your own gut reactions as to whom you like and trust.	• You will have to show potential tenants your property at their convenience, interview them and trust your judgement. Their references may be the only concrete evidence you can draw upon in the vetting process. Make a few telephone calls to check their validity.
• You will be at viewings so you can get an idea why people may not want to rent the property. You may be able to act on their comments and make it more lettable.	• You may find the private letting process slower than using an agent who has more resources at their disposal.
• There are a number of basic ready-made legal contracts, such as the Assured Shorthold Tenancy Agreement, which you can purchase from good stationers, to cut down your administration and legal costs.	• You will need to ensure all of the services are transferred into the tenant's name and check all meter readings are correct so they are billed appropriately.
• You can ensure that any repairs that need to be made to the property can be carried out by contractors whom you trust, at a price you negotiate and to a standard you are happy with.	• You will have to deal with repairs yourself and swiftly, as soon as things go wrong. This may mean cancelling a weekend away because a boiler has exploded and receiving calls at 10.00 p.m. on Sunday evenings.
• You inspect the property yourself so you can be aware of anything that needs to be dealt with before it becomes a crisis.	• You personally will be responsible for collecting rents and deposits, and handling disputes over when these sums are paid and how.
	• Having an independent party conduct an inventory can be costly, but it is essential. At the end of the tenancy, you will need to replenish any broken or damaged items from the inventory using the liable tenant's deposit. For this reason it is wise to remove any items that are more valuable than the sum total of the deposit.
	• You will need to organise for the property to be maintained – this means employing reliable cleaners to vacuum and dust any communal areas, and painters and decorators to freshen up the interior and exterior of the property when necessary.

USING A FULL MANAGEMENT SERVICE

PROS	CONS
• An agent is experienced in how best to prepare your property for rent and should know how to target the appropriate market directly.	• Agents cost money (see commission costs on page 90).
• An agent will have a ready-made database of clients to whom to market the property and can place adverts in specialist publications on your behalf.	• Agents can often delay the payment of rental income to the landlord, which can be frustrating and inhibit cash flow.
• An agent will undertake all viewings, so you don't have to.	• Some agents are not sufficiently set up to deal with out-of-hours emergency repairs.
• An agent will verify the status of would-be tenants' references, run a credit check and confirm their employers' details.	• Just because you are paying for a service doesn't necessarily mean that you will be 100% happy with it.
• An agent will provide a signed contract from the tenant.	• Agents may commit the landlord to large repair bills without prior warning or consultation.
• After your initial gas checks, some agents will ensure that both your gas and electrical appliances are checked at regular intervals at your own cost.	• Agents can spring a fee for additional 'extras' on landlords such as rates for advertising. Always check what is included in your fee and never assume services are automatic.
• An agent will arrange all minor repairs and redecoration of the property as and when required, again at your own cost.	• Some agents offer an inspections service, which is negotiable depending on how many times a year you would like them to check the property for deterioration. Don't assume that regular inspections are always part of the package.
• An agent will act as a mediator between the landlord and the tenant.	
• An agent will collect the rent from your tenant and ensure that it is paid every month. If a tenant fails to pay, the agent will carry out procedures for eviction, rental recovery and finding a new tenant, although this process can take many months.	
• An agent will provide support and advice if a dispute arises with a tenant.	
• If you ask an agent to manage multiple properties, you may be able to negotiate a reduced fee.	
• If you place multiple lets with an agent you will receive a monthly statement with every property listed on it and a consolidated return, which makes life easier when you calculate your cash flow.	
• An agent is able to provide specialist insurance policies, which provide extra protection to the landlord at an additional cost:	
a) Rental guarantee insurance – guarantees part or all of your rent in the event of a disappearing tenant. This usually costs about 3% of the monthly rental income.	
b) Legal costs insurance – covers a legal dispute up to £50,000 for approximately £5 per week.	
c) Emergency repair insurance – protects against large repair bills for approximately £5 per week.	

CHAPTER SUMMARY

1 Organise your site as soon as contracts are exchanged and find your materials and contractors as soon as the property sale is complete.

2 Don't take the role of project manager lightly. Be sure you know what the job entails before you decide whether you can do it yourself or need to hire a professional.

3 Give your workmen precise instructions and know exactly what you want done before you ask for any quotes.

4 Draft an accurate schedule of all on-site work so that materials and tradesmen are booked for the right time.

5 Be super-organised if you are managing more than one property on-site. Be careful not to lose track of separate schedules and budgets.

6 Be aware of your responsibilities as a site owner and as a landlord.

7 Don't dismiss the idea of a managing agent before you have found out what services they offer and the fees they charge.

8 Get some financial advice and don't overstretch yourself by taking on multiple projects.

DEVELOPING YOUR PROPERTY

DESIGN BASICS

Choosing the right spec and design for your market
Calling in the experts
Working with what you already have
Spatial solutions
Maximising the appeal of your 'buy to let'

Choosing the right spec and design for your market

How you design and present your property will strongly influence how well it is likely to do once it is on the market. To get it right, you *must* target your design directly to your potential buyer.

A recent survey by estate agents Bradford & Bingley estimated that the average viewing lasts twenty minutes, but that prospective buyers tend to make up their minds within five or ten minutes or even sometimes before they ring the doorbell, hence the importance of kerb appeal. Now that buyers are pickier than ever, you have very little time to make the right impression. The key to getting it right is knowing your market and exactly what they want.

Different types of buyers lead different lifestyles and have diverse expectations of what they want from a home. Young professionals, for example, want properties in locations with good transport links, shops and nightlife, while families tend to prefer houses rather than flats, and consider gardens a high priority. It is therefore essential to pinpoint your market and renovate your property accordingly in order to achieve your top selling price and maximum profit.

CASE STUDY

Shoreditch: Creating an expensive look

Merchant banker Tallat Mukhtar bought a 900 square foot shell in Shoreditch. He hoped to turn it into a luxury loft for a young professional market and sell at a profit of £100,000. Tallat worked full time in the city but planned to do all of the work himself, with the help of his brother.

PROJECT COSTS

Cost of property	£220,000
Renovation budget	£30,000
Target resale price	£350,000
Anticipated pre-tax profit	**£100,000**

the plan
The Shoreditch market is a unique mix of high-earning city slickers and creative types. They have swapped traditional homes for urban lofts with big open spaces filled with daylight as many of them work from home and enjoy entertaining. One of the key rooms to get right for these buyers is the kitchen as they have little time to prepare food and love entertaining. Another key room is the bathroom.

The bare shell in Tallat's loft apartment provided the perfect opportunity to create a truly contemporary interior.

Shoreditch specialises in loft living and the competition is fierce. There is no shortage of beautiful contemporary properties for sale and the standards are high. The most desirable and expensive lofts are converted from old commercial properties and many developers have retained the original features and character of the building. To achieve his top selling price, Tallat's completed development would have to stand out above the rest and, as a new developer, he was taking a huge risk taking on such a challenge when his property was of a relatively standard size. He would need to pay particular attention to detail and the finish of the loft, particularly the kitchen, to achieve top asking price.

sarah's advice

The look Tallat needed to pull off was expensive, but he had only £30,000 to do the job. I would not normally advise increasing your budget at this stage as it eats into your profit. But without the extra funds, Tallat would not be able to achieve the type of finish his market required. He upped his budget to £50,000.

SEE ALSO	
p116	More on Tallat's project: Expert help
p38	Identifying your target market

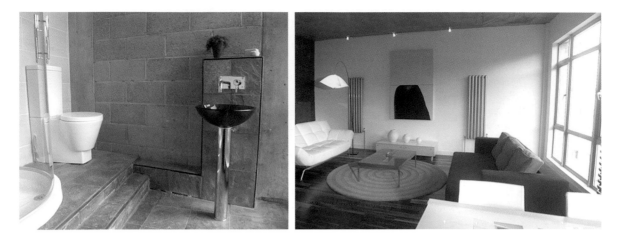

Left: The fake limestone tiles in Tallat's en-suite bathroom were effective without blowing the budget. Right: The industrial style radiators and concrete ceilings in Tallat's loft were softened by the lighting scheme and warm materials and textures.

Tallat planned to spend one-fifth of his budget on the kitchen. However, partway through the project he decided that he would like to keep the property as a 'buy to let'. For this reason I advised him to reconsider his intended finishes because fragile high-spec touches would become tarnished and worn in a rental apartment. He would still need to create the look, but items would need to be very hard-wearing or cheap enough to be regularly replaced. This is not as difficult as you may think. Whatever your budget, you can create a really expensive look by using ideas from top-end manufacturers and incorporating them into your own design. To save money think laterally, design carefully and do lots of research and relentless shopping around.

SMALL BUDGETS, BIG IDEAS

All developments need to incorporate good design but memorable design ideas need not cost a fortune. Simply include elements that will make your property stand out from all the viewings as the one to buy:

- Use a sliding door to create a flexible and heightened sense of space. This can be even more effective, although more expensive, if you create a cavity wall the door can slide into.

- Create a luxury look in the bathroom by installing two wash basins or a double-sized shower. Add inexpensive subtle lights to create mood and glamour effectively at the switch of a button. Consider industrial and raw materials, like Indian slate, which are fashionable and often cheaper than those with a more polished finish.

- Remember, it doesn't have to be real. Limestone-effect tiles in an en-suite bathroom, for example, provide a similar effect to the real thing, but won't stain. Fakes are more convincing when mixed with some high-spec finishes, so consider balancing budget buys with a few expensive touches.

- Balance textures, mixing the rough with the smooth.

- Choose furniture that appeals to your target market.

how the project progressed

Tallat saved money on the kitchen by buying a flat-packed design from the high street for just £1,000. He then made it look more exclusive and luxurious by adding an expensive durable granite worktop, and good-quality appliances that would last and create the right impression alongside his fashionable fixtures and fittings.

If he had been fitting the kitchen to sell to the top end of the young professional market I would have advised he considered some cutting-edge design elements.

CUTTING-EDGE KITCHENS

Bear in mind that style statements of the moment date quickly. This is great if you are selling immediately but not so desirable in a 'buy to let':

- The current trends in kitchen design include 'floating' kitchens – underlit units suspended from the wall without legs or plinths. Simple, unpanelled plain-fronted units add to this sleek effect.

- A combination of raw materials such as granite, glass and stainless steel is standard.

- Beautifully designed, state-of-the-art appliances like glass-fronted fridges, oversized hobs and seamless sinks never fail to wow any buyer.

- An integrated coffee machine, a high-tech steam oven and showerhead-style taps are the must-have kitchen gadgets right now.

the outcome

After almost six months of hard work Tallat finished the loft and it looked amazing. It was an impressive product and he had used his budget well to create the bright, spacious feel of a loft that would appeal to his market. Fake limestone tiles in the en-suite bathroom were effective without blowing the budget while a wall cladded with Indian slate gave a sense of warmth and luxury. The industrial-style radiators and concrete ceilings were softened by the loft's lighting scheme; the furniture in the apartment was contemporary yet welcoming and perfect for entertaining – ideal for his target market of young professionals.

If he had sold the property, Tallat would have made a profit of £110,000. But Tallat decided he wanted to rent rather than sell and it is currently let for £450 per week. ✏

SUMMARY OF PROJECT COSTS

	ORIGINAL SUMS	FINAL SUMS
Cost of property	£220,000	£220,000
Renovation budget (including legal fees)	£30,000	£45,000
Total investment	£250,000	£265,000
Target resale value	£350,000	£375,000
Projected profit	**£100,000** **(excluding rise in market)**	**£110,000** **(including rise in market)**

Market Harborough: Focusing on the important issues

Next-door neighbours Jamie Whitcombe and Jane Albon embarked on their first development by taking on a Victorian terraced house in Market Harborough after Jane was forced to leave her job designing clothes and Jamie was made redundant.

Jane and Jamie spent three months searching for the right property and eventually settled on a developer's dream. The house, although untouched for twenty years, was structurally sound, but in need of total modernisation. The property needed a new heating system, a new kitchen and complete rewiring. As well as extensive damp work it needed redecorating throughout and the large garden at the back of the house needed landscaping.

Jamie remortgaged his family home to finance his share in this project and Jane invested her savings. Neither had any money to fall back on, so they had to bring this project in on time and on budget. To do so, Jane and Jamie intended to work on-site full time and get the property back on the market in just three months.

Jane thought that the property would appeal to young professionals, but there was evidence all around to suggest that their actual market was young families. Set within easy reach of the town centre, the house is opposite a common and beside a children's playground. Renovating the property with a family in mind would therefore be the best option for Jamie and Jane.

PROJECT COSTS

Cost of property	£100,000
Renovation budget (including fees)	£11,000
Target resale price	£135,000
Anticipated pre-tax profit	**£24,000**

the plan

The property was a two-up two-down end-of-terrace with a classic Victorian layout. On the ground floor, there were two reasonably sized reception rooms – the living room at the front of the house and a spacious dining room at the back. There was also a small back addition with a kitchen, pantry and outside loo. Upstairs, there was a double bedroom at the front of the house, a smaller second bedroom to the rear and a bathroom in the back addition. Jane and Jamie planned to leave the layout upstairs as it stood and give the interior some TLC, especially the bathroom. Downstairs, however, was another story.

Feeling that the house didn't offer enough living space, Jamie had plans to convert the cellars to create two further reception rooms. The basement had remained untouched since the house was built. Jamie had little building experience and I was unsure whether he realised the extent of the work and costs he would be taking on.

SEE ALSO

Identifying your target market   p 38

Jane and Jamie successfully transformed this living room with a cool, calm palette of colours and textures.

To convert the cellars properly would cost a fortune. Jane and Jamie had allocated just £500 and intended to give the space a cosmetic makeover.

sarah's advice

My first concern with this plan was that a half job would only highlight the problem of damp in the cellars. A quick-fix solution like this costs money and, by not doing the job properly, is a serious risk. Tell-tale signs can appear quickly and lack of building regulations can easily hold up a sale. Jamie should have been spending money where it was needed and as efficiently as possible – but whatever work he decided to do, it must be done properly. With a budget of only £11,000 to complete all of the work on this development, any money they planned to spend in the basement would be put to much better use upstairs.

My second concern with the cellar conversion was that it would not be an effective space solution. Jamie was convinced that adding two rooms downstairs would add value to the house – but the original layout already worked. It is not wise to increase space in a property if it will not increase the market price and be practical for the market. A family wanting two bedrooms would be unlikely to want four reception rooms.

how the project progressed

The project got off to a good start with Jane seemingly on top of the schedule. However during the refurbishment her ideas evolved and her plans changed somewhat. Despite throwing out the original bathroom suite, she was keen to keep some of the other original features. This included the fireplace in the dining room … which she wanted moved to the living room. Planning on doing this, Jamie ripped out the fireplace from the dining room, but they changed their minds again and ended up removing it from the property entirely. Jamie then built a new wooden surround to fit in its place in the dining room.

One area where Jane wasn't changing her mind was the kitchen. In an attempt to create more space in this room Jane and Jamie planned to move the dining room

SEE ALSO

p 116 Complying with building regulations

p 121 Working with what you already have

Jane and Jamie decided to keep the structure of the kitchen and use the space where the loo had been planned for storage. However, this felt like a wasted space and I wish they had taken my advice from the beginning. If Jamie and Jane got rid of the loo and the boiler cupboard, they could open up the kitchen completely and add big French doors looking out onto the garden and make it feel twice the size.

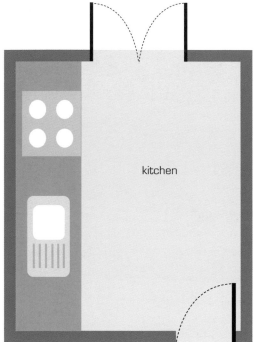

kitchen

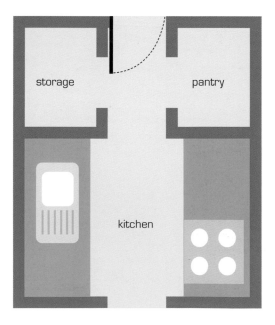

storage

pantry

kitchen

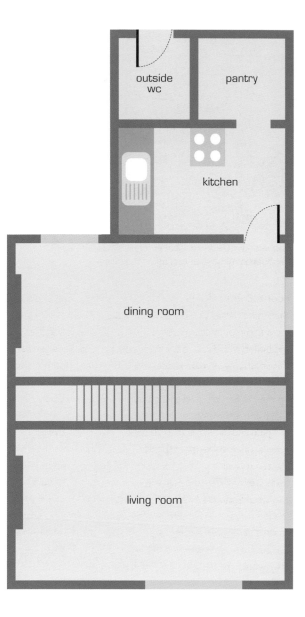

outside wc

pantry

kitchen

dining room

living room

Jamle and Jane's new kitchen looked fresh and contemporary, but the lack of wall cupboards minimised storage space in this room.

door and make it slightly wider, which would give a more open-plan feel through to the kitchen. They also planned to change the layout at the back of the kitchen by moving the outside loo inside into the pantry. The space opposite would be used for the boiler with a new back door going out into the garden. I wasn't convinced that this solution would be successful. This two-bedroom terraced house didn't need an extra bathroom. If they got rid of the loo and the boiler cupboard they could open up the kitchen completely and put in big French doors, thereby maximizing the space and garden potential.

Jane and Jamie decided to ignore my advice and go ahead with moving the downstairs loo, but after spending time and money on new drains and plumbing, they started to wonder whether the space was actually big enough to squeeze a loo into. I was worried that the pair were wasting money on a loo that was too small to use and would ruin the layout of their kitchen along the way. Opening up the kitchen and fitting double doors would have been more effective and appeal to the family market, despite Jane being adamant that this house was for young professionals. Furthermore, if they ditched the loo and cupboard, the money they would save would pay for new French doors.

five weeks later

Five weeks into the project and while downstairs was still in chaos, upstairs was starting to take shape. Here, the pair were on time and within budget because they had taken on doing more and more of the work themselves.

Jamie was still determined to transform the two cellars but I was pleased to see that he had put his plans on hold until he got the rest of the house sorted out. First on the list was the kitchen. Having consulted a building inspector six weeks before starting the project, Jamie asked him to come back to sign off on the alterations that had been made. However, the inspector was unhappy with the doorway Jamie had bricked up from the dining room to the kitchen.

He also had serious doubts that the space they had created for the downstairs loo was big enough. To adhere to building regulations a loo situated next to a kitchen

Although Jane and Jamie could have saved money by recycling this perfectly good bathroom suite, they created a great look with their finished scheme.

must have its own basin and there simply wasn't room for this. This was a major setback for Jane and Jamie who now discovered that they had wasted money on plumbing and drainage for a loo they could not have.

nine weeks later

Nine weeks into the project and Jamie was still keen to get cracking on the cellar. However, his plumber and electrician refused to work in the basement because the rooms were so damp. Jamie should have been spending time finishing the rest of the house as there was still lots to be done upstairs and the back garden had hardly been touched. But despite all of this, Jamie went ahead, installed a window and started to dig out the floor himself. I admired his determination but this job would usually take a professional company weeks. However, on speaking to the local authority,. Jamie discovered that the house had no foundations and he was finally forced to abandon the cellar idea, forget about the £200 he had spent on the window and concentrate on getting the house finished.

Jamie now pushed the project towards the finish line, with Jane keeping him on track. And their luck seemed to change. Jane and Jamie managed to sell half of their huge back garden for £15,000 – a true triumph. Negotiating your way to profit is what property developing is all about. Realising the capital in any development, be it with surplus land or adjoining buildings, can be a great way of making cash. By getting the best price for the extra space in the garden, Jane and Jamie had now covered the cost of their entire development. Anything they made now would be a bonus.

the outcome

The pair worked hard and came in on time and amazingly on budget. In just twelve weeks Jamie and Jane's house was transformed from a tired, old end-of-terrace into a modern family home. The colours Jane had chosen were cool and calm and she had harmonised the house with neutral tones and textures.

They had created a dining room big enough for a family or young professionals and by opening up into the kitchen, they had cleverly linked both areas, although I still thought it would have been better to have taken out the whole wall. The original feature fireplace that had been removed ended up by being replaced by a cheaper home-made surround and, although it looked good, getting rid of the old one was probably a shame.

The kitchen was modern, simple and just what buyers look for. The stainless steel appliances worked well, but in order to keep their costs down, Jane had decided against fitting wall units in here. I was concerned that lack of storage could put some buyers off.

The back door opened up on to a successful patio area but I couldn't help thinking that Jane and Jamie could have provided a better view of the garden had they fitted a larger pair of doors so as to really appreciate it from the inside.

Upstairs, although the original bathroom hadn't really needed replacing, Jamie and Jane's contemporary suite looked great. The separate shower would also impress buyers. The back bedroom and master bedroom were finished in a neutral style and the wood floors finished the look off brilliantly. Jane had also done a great job dressing the house with furniture borrowed from a friend's store although she need not have spent money having both curtains *and* blinds made.

Jane's £1500 spent on blinds left nothing in the budget for dressing the house. I also felt that £600 spent on the back door was a little excessive and that the money Jamie had spent on the cellar window was wasted. However, Jane and Jamie made massive cuts in other areas to bring their budget under control. They saved £400 on their kitchen budget, didn't use any of their budget for the garden and did lots of work themselves to save on labour.

They had had a budget of £11,000 to develop this property, including all fees and expenses, but they had managed to save in so many areas, which is what property developing is all about. Their final spend was only £500 over the original budget. Spending so much money on the cellar window was one mistake – Jamie could have used this money elsewhere to knock through the kitchen, and just added some shelving to the cellar and tried at no cost to make this space more appealing.

Jane and Jamie had set an asking price at the start of this project of £135,000, which seemed a little optimistic to me, but with a house that ended up looking this good and needing no work doing to it, they could get lucky. ✎

SUMMARY OF PROJECT COSTS

	ORIGINAL SUMS	FINAL SUMS	
Cost of property	£100,000	£100,000	
Renovation budget (including legal fees)	£11,000	£11,500	
Total investment	£111,000	£111,500	
Target resale value	£135,000	£135,000	
		+ £15,000	for selling back garden
Projected profit	**£24,000**	**£38,500**	

Calling in the experts

Whatever the size and scale of your project, there are always times when you need a little help.

Before purchasing your property, you should have assessed the extent of the repairs, work and decoration required to make it perfect for you or your market. Don't be daunted by major building works or extensive repairs, just take responsibility to make the property safe and sound first and foremost. If you have done your calculations correctly, you should have the resources to get the job done properly.

It is crucial to know your limitations when it comes to property developing. Time is money so it is important to recognise when you need to hire someone to help you do some of the work. A good tradesperson is a busy one, so start looking early on in your project. This will avoid delays and give you time to make the right choices.

Choosing your builder

Choosing a good builder is essential to the smooth and swift running of any development. The bottom line is that you need to build a reputable team you can rely on and trust to get the job done. This will stand you in good stead now and in any future developments. To go about finding the right team start with a recommendation or referral. You may have a friend, family member or professional acquaintance who has recently had a job carried out on schedule, within budget and to a high standard. If so, check the job yourself and get an idea of the builder's track record. If you like what you see, call the builder to arrange a time to meet and discuss a quote.

Another option is to contact the appropriate trades body for details of contractors in your area. The Federation of Master Builders and the Guild of Master Craftsmen, for example, encourage their members to work and practise to a certain standard. While this is still no guarantee, it is more reliable than plucking a number at random from a directory like the *Yellow Pages*.

When you've got some builders' names, ask three to quote for the job:
- Prepare a detailed list of works you want done throughout the property. Be specific and give as much detail as possible. Give a copy to each builder and ask for a quote.
- Encourage each builder to submit an itemised quote for each stage of the project and a breakdown of materials. When you receive an itemised quote, you will able to see where and how to reduce costs – if necessary by deciding to do more of the project yourself. You can try haggling, but be aware that if you force the price down too far it may not be possible for the builder to make his profit. You may come unstuck at some point in the project as there is no reason why he should work on your project for nothing.

SARAH SUGGESTS ... 'Think carefully about who to employ. Who did you get on with? Who seems best equipped to do the job or has the most relevant experience? Don't automatically opt for the cheapest quote, and double-check that nothing has been missed out from the spec.'

Don't be embarrassed to ask for references or to suggest you see examples of a builder's work. In addition, check that any contractor you find is able to supply the relevant paperwork and guarantees for reroofing, rewiring, plumbing and damp work. Confirm your method of payment and check that the builder has his own insurance.

Finally, check the availability of the builder. Never employ one who has too many other commitments at the same time as your job. You want someone who will be committed to your site and ensure the work is done when you need it done. You don't want your builder to overstretch himself, you want him to help keep you on schedule.

Once you have decided who to employ, add your builder's figures to your original list of works. Be thorough and methodical. If you leave anything off at this stage, it will cost you time and money when you ask the builder to add the job on. Be detailed, accurate and clear about the works and the time-scale from the outset, to minimise misunderstandings that could cost you dearly.

If you are employing an architect or a project manager, they will often have a team of contractors and builders they are used to working with. If a solid working relationship between your manager and a building firm is already established, a number of headaches are theoretically alleviated. However, never take this as given. It is advisable that you meet the builder who will be working on your property.

Before any work starts on-site, make sure your tradesmen can offer you a written contract upfront confirming all the details of the job.

Employing an architect

Architects are trained problem solvers and skilled visualisers. If you are planning a job that is too big or too complicated for you and your builder, it is time to get one on board. You should certainly employ an architect if you intend to carry out any major architectural or structural changes to your property (see box overleaf). They will tell you whether what you are proposing is possible and how to achieve it, and will advise on the best approach for the property and your purse strings. They will also advise on how to achieve more light, space or rooms in your property, all of which can add value to it. Their recommendations and results can be incredible, but their skills do come at a cost, of course.

Architect's rates vary as much as any other professionals. If you want to hire one just to draw up plans for planning permission, they will charge around £55 per hour for this service. An architect who works with you on the project from concept to completion is likely to charge anything from 10% upwards of the total cost of your renovation works.

TIP
Make sure you are happy and confident with your team. One easy way is to suggest that your project manager puts the work out to tender. He will gather more than one quote from different contractors. You can then make an informed judgement from the results as to who you want to employ.

Even if you don't employ an architect, if you are making structural changes you will need to enlist the services of a structural surveyor. For insurance reasons, a structural surveyor will generally need to be employed directly by you, although they will also work closely with your architect, project manager and builder.

Before investing, be objective and make sure that the proposed architectural/structural changes will increase the market value of your property by an amount that both covers the cost of the work and provides you with an additional profit for your efforts. If it does, go ahead and apply for any necessary planning permission.

FINDING AN ARCHITECT

- As with builders and other contractors, it is always good to have a recommendation. Ask friends and professional contacts whether they know of anyone who has recently used an architects' practice whose residential work they were particularly happy with.

- Seek advice from the RIBA (Royal Institute of British Architects). The organisation offers a telephone and internet service that helps match an RIBA-registered architect to the job you propose.

- Alternatively, scout the internet for architects' sites and browse glossy interiors books in the library. You are looking for a firm specialising in residential work, whose style you like and you can envisage improving your development.

- Next, make a call to several practices and arrange some meetings. You want to get an idea of costs and see whether you can communicate clearly, and exchange ideas, with the architect on a level you are happy with. You will also want to check their availability upfront, so that you don't commit to them, only to discover you may incur delays while they finish another project.

HOW TO APPLY FOR PLANNING PERMISSION

If you employ an architect, they will generally apply for planning permission on your behalf. If you decide not to employ an architect, here's what you need to do:

1 Phone the council for a planning application form.

2 Draw up relevant scale drawings of your existing and proposed dwelling according to your proposed work. These will be likely to include elevations and basic floor plans. These drawings generally need to be 1:100 in scale and 100% accurate, so don't even think of trying to do this yourself unless you are totally confident!

3 Submit the plans and application form to the council with the appropriate fee (currently £95).

4 Await the council's acknowledgement of receipt of application.

5 The council will write to the properties in the immediate locality and/or post notice on your property about the proposed changes. These home owners have 21 days in which to go to the public library or the council to see the plans for themselves and lodge an objection.

6 If the council receives more than two objections then the decision will go to a committee where a decision about the proposal will be made.

7 Planning permission will be either granted or refused. If refused, you have the option of taking the council's decision to appeal but be warned that there is no guarantee that the appeal's decision will be any different. It is more sensible instead to listen to the council's comments, revise your plans and resubmit your application.

8 If planning permission is granted and, during work being carried out on the property, the owner wishes to make any minor changes to the original and approved plans, they must submit the amendment – generally via a drawing – to the planning department. A planning officer, probably the one who dealt with the original application, will decide whether or not these are significant changes requiring submission of a further planning application.

9 If the council feels that the proposed changes are not significant enough, then work can start on the second phase. If it considers they are significant, however, and you are still running the site then the council has the power to issue an enforcement notice to stop the work and/or insist on the submission of a retrospective planning application.

10 On receipt of this, the owner has a legal obligation to stop work until the appropriate planning permission is gained. If permission is not granted, they must undo whatever work has been done so that it complies with their original application, even if this means pulling down thousands of pounds worth of expensive and skilled work.

11 The Building Regulations Officer, based in the planning department, is also in a position to place a stop notice should your work not comply with current building regulations (see overleaf).

Complying with building regulations

Building regulations ensure that any work you do on the property is safe and legal. Although it may not be necessary to apply for planning permission to carry out work on your development, any work must always adhere to current building regulations:

- Consult the Building Regulations Officer at the local council planning office *before* embarking on any building work. Ask for a copy of their guidelines and relevant application forms, depending on the amount of work you are carrying out.
- Submit the appropriate paperwork.
- Expect a Building Regulations Officer to visit your site to make sure it is running in accordance with the guidelines.
- You can start work without them, but at your own risk. Any work that does not comply must be changed and officers do have the power to shut down any site that does not comply or that they consider unsafe.
- A Building Regulations Approval Certificate will be issued by the department on the satisfactory completion of works. You will need this when you come to sell the property.

TIP

Consult the Building Regulations department early on in your development so that you don't start to carry out work that does not comply with building regulations.

SARAH SUGGESTS ... 'Never carry out any work on property that fails to comply with building regulations. Not only is it a criminal offence, but if the extra work is spotted by your purchaser's solicitor or surveyor in the paperwork, they may advise their client to insist on a price reduction or, worse still, not to purchase the property at all. It is therefore never worth the risk.'

Shoreditch: Expert help

The importance of employing the right people for the job, applying for planning permission and adhering to building regulations is well illustrated by merchant banker Tallat Mukhtar's Shoreditch development, already encountered earlier in this chapter.

Tallat was keen to renovate his property himself and to sell it at top price to a young professional market. Despite having no experience as a developer and little knowledge of DIY, he was keen to be his own project manager, architect and builder while working full time. He hoped the project would take three months to complete and took two weeks off work at the beginning of the project to kick-start the work.

The shell came fitted with basic plumbing and electricity but no dividing walls. Tallat began by designing the loft space and spent a great deal of time drawing his own plans to submit with his planning application. In his design he included an

SEE ALSO

More on Tallat's project: Creating an expensive look   p 102

open-plan kitchen and living area, two bedrooms and two bathrooms, an arrangement I agreed in theory would add the most value to the property. However, the loft was on the third floor of the building and the only fire exit allowed for in Tallat's design was through the open-plan kitchen and living area. This would mean that from the bedroom, the occupants would have to walk through a habitable room to get to a staircase. I knew this would not comply with fire regulations and suggested building a wall to partition off the hallway to provide a means of escape. Either way, Tallat and his brother started to erect the metal studwork to divide up the space.

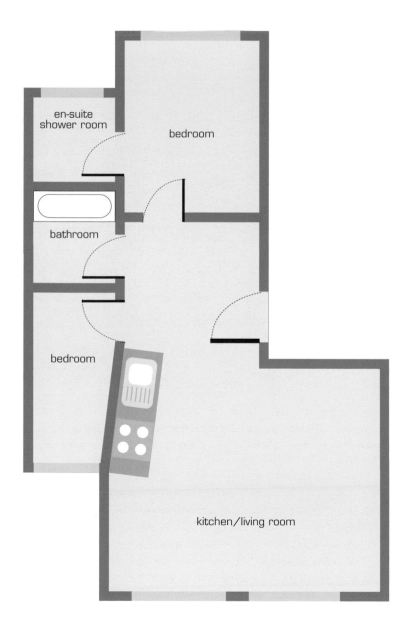

Tallat designed his loft space to contain an open-plan kitchen and living area, two bedrooms and two bathrooms. While this arrangement would add most value to the property in theory, it would not comply with building regulations as it meant that the only fire exit would be accessed through the open-plan kitchen/living area. In other words, the occupants would have to walk through a habitable room to reach a staircase.

I recommended that Tallat redesign the area and build a wall to separate the living area from the entrance hall. Fire doors were fitted off the hallway to access the bedrooms. Tallat could have saved a lot of time, money and labour by finding out about building regulations first before designing his loft – make sure you do the same.

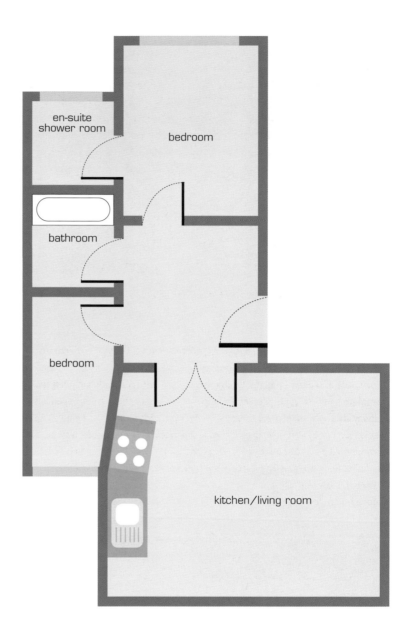

Tallat submitted his building regulations application and plans but the amateur drawings did not make the grade. They were not to scale, did not include nearly enough detail and he had failed to seek advice about fire regulations. He now had to redesign the loft to address this fire issue and did end up building a wall to separate the living area from the entrance hall. Hallway fire doors would be fitted off this to access the bedrooms. This was a long process as Tallat and his brother found it quite difficult to work from Tallat's plans. There was confusion as to whether they were working to the right proportions and dimensions when they were erecting the studwork and ordering materials from the local builder's merchants.

Dividing up an empty shell effectively can be harder than you think. As Tallat found out, it's all in the planning.

To avoid making Tallat's mistake yourself, contact the planning department early on in your project. Save time and energy by employing an architect to help you design your space and draw up plans. Doing this himself left Tallat only eight weeks to complete the rest of his project. To help move things along he employed a builder halfway through the project to work on the loft with him in the evenings and on weekends. Time is money so recognising when it is more cost effective to pay someone else to do the work more quickly and efficiently is essential.

Tallat felt the strain of trying to hold down a full-time job in the city and project manage his own development. It was time to call in some professional help. But before he could hand things over, Tallat had to find the right project manager. It took

Tallat's project ground to a halt when his project manager let him down, costing him valuable time and money.

him six weeks to appoint Denis. But on Denis's first day on-site, his plasterer failed to show up and Tallat turned up at the development to find that work had ground to a halt. Tallat asked Denis to leave. He felt that the contractor's prices were astronomical and didn't feel he could trust anyone to project manage the job the way he wanted it done. Note that contractors often charge a higher fee to rescue a project midway through a development, often because they see part of the job as catching up to speed and putting someone else's work right.

Tallat decided to project manage the development himself and bring in contractors to do the work when he needed them. In reality, this meant that every day, after a hard slog at the merchant bank, Tallat had to pay a visit to the site to make sure things went to plan. He spent the rest of his time sourcing fixtures and fittings between meetings, but with his development running over schedule, he had to get things done.

Five months into the project, Tallat made a life-changing decision. He left his lucrative job in merchant banking to focus on property developing as his new career. Being on-site full time meant he could get the development finished and concentrate on every detail. He learnt a huge amount from his first experience as a developer and now has a contacts book full of contractors' telephone numbers, ready for his next project.

Working with what you already have

When you purchase a property to develop that is in a bad state of repair, it is tempting to rip everything out and start again. Salvaging what you have, however, can not only save you money but also appeal to your market.

Period features

If you have bought a period property to develop it is likely that your market will be looking to buy a home with character. Think before you rip out any original features. If they are damaged, can they be restored? Check what is waiting to be rediscovered beneath 'modern improvements' and see what you can do to save them:

cornicing
If it is damaged or crumbling, you can hire a specialist to make a mould of a good part of the cornice to repeat the pattern in plaster in the damaged area.

fireplaces
Good stone masons or marble restorers can restore chipped or broken surrounds – always get a quote before you commission one. If the fireplace has been painted and you think it would look better in its original wood finish, carefully strip and treat it.

floors
Exposing and maintaining original flooring utilises what you already have and can add real value to a property. To revive wooden floors give them a vigorous scrub with a mix of one part turpentine, one part methylated spirits and one part vinegar. Finish with two or more coats of floor polish.

doors
If you have a period property, you can buy a wooden moulding kit to make fire door blanks blend in better with panelled doors.

roll-top baths
If you find in your property a cast-iron or roll-top bath that looks like it has seen better days, think before you skip it! The original is much more desirable than modern plastic. Be warned, never attempt to move a roll-top bath yourself. They are very heavy and you could damage your property as well as your back!

A tatty bath can look like new again with the help of an enamelling kit and shiny new taps.

An inexpensive kitchen makeover

If you buy a property with a good-quality but tired kitchen, updating it without replacing it may take pressure off your budget, and a well-presented kitchen will always help sell your property.

Banish 1980s oak without replacing your kitchen units, for example, by painting them to give a more modern look. First sand the varnished oak, apply a base coat of multi-purpose primer and finish with a good-quality eggshell paint. Finish the look by adding new modern chrome or brushed-steel handles – many homeware stores have ranges that look luxurious with an affordable price tag.

Paint walls and ceiling a clean neutral colour to brighten and freshen the room. If your tiles look tired, then consider retiling, regrouting or freshening the grouting with a whitening pen, available from most DIY stores. Don't forget the floor either. Retile, lay a fashionable linoleum or use floor paint on sanded boards. Lastly, add a new modern blind at the window and place some fresh herbs or a bottle of expensive-looking olive oil on your scrubbed-up work surface.

Spatial solutions

A large number of British houses are spatially challenged, but people buying homes still expect as much space as they can get for their money. So, what is the answer?

Because half of Britain's housing stock was built before World War II, the average living room is a mere 15 × 13 feet (4.5 × 4 metres). To make a limited area feel spacious you need good design to maximise how it looks. You cannot make space physically larger without knocking down walls or building an extension, but you certainly can make it *feel* bigger (see table opposite).

Decreasing a sense of space

Sometimes, vast open spaces can feel *too* large. They make us feel vulnerable and unable to relax. The answer is to cordon off sections visually, using colour and furniture.

A rich enveloping colour will add warmth to a large space and strong, dark colours bring walls in. This can be particularly useful if you have a room with an irregular shape. A long narrow room can appear squarer, for example, if you paint the furthest, smallest wall a dark colour to bring it closer to the eye. Strong colour on the long walls, on the other hand, give a long, thin corridor effect.

Use larger, more decadent pieces of furniture to zone specific areas within an overlarge room.

TIP

In a very tiny room without a window, it is sometimes good to break the rule of using pale colours to increase a sense of space and go for a rich, strong colour instead. In a loo, for example, this can look stunning, but you have to be very sure about it. If in doubt adopt this approach for your own home only, rather than for a development where you want to appeal to the broadest section of the market possible.

CREATING THE ILLUSION OF SPACE

COLOUR

- Pale, light colours help increase a sense of space. Imagine if you painted the walls, ceiling and floor of a room totally white – the eye would see no limits. Obviously this is not what you are aiming to do, but it does demonstrate that if you think light and bright, you can increase the sense of space.

FLOORING

- Laying the same flooring throughout a property opens up the space.
- Carpets and rugs, particularly dark-coloured ones, absorb light with their texture and hold it like a sponge. For a small space choose hard, shiny floorcoverings like wood, resin, tile or slate. These materials will bounce light and sound, making the space feel larger than it really is.
- The direction in which you lay a floor or pattern can have an impact. Vertical lines accentuate length and depth, horizontal lines accentuate width.
- Removing the skirting from a room does increase the sense of space but you need an exceptional, and very contemporary, finish to carry off this look.

CEILINGS

- High ceilings increase the sense of space whereas the shiny, swirly patterns of an Artexed ceiling visually drip and make it feel lower than it really is. Plaster and skim over Artex to visually push that ceiling back up again.

WINDOWS

- The more daylight that fills a room, the more space there seems to be. So where you can, add a window to a dark or small room, or increase the scale of an existing one.
- Keep window treatments clean and uncluttered. Big bolts of fabric and swathes of curtains fill up visual space and cut down the amount of light that filters through the windows.
- Views of outside space expand our immediate surroundings and take them beyond the room. If you are deprived of a view use an old Japanese trick. Place an eye-catching object just the other side of the window, such as a willow tree, a brightly coloured sculpture or planter. Your eye will be led to the object, thereby extending the sense of space by proportion and line.

MIRRORS AND PICTURES

- Use mirrors and pictures to reflect light. Place them strategically to visually push out narrow walls in a long thin room, or use them like windows, reflecting corners and vistas of a room and making the whole space feel bigger.
- If you have a low ceiling, try placing a large picture in the middle of the most dominant wall. The picture will act as an eye magnet, drawing your eyes to the picture instead of the low ceiling.

PATTERN AND SHAPE

- Wallpaper with vertical stripes draws the eye upwards, increasing the sense of height.
- Dado rails and wallpaper with horizontal lines visually increase width.
- In a low cramped stairwell, use long, thin vertically striped wallpaper to balance the heavy broad bands of timber as you travel up the stairs.

FURNITURE

- Generally, you should only ever place pieces of furniture that are in proportion to the scale of the room. A large sofa in a small living room, for example, will swamp the room and make it feel cramped.
- Move the furniture slightly away from the walls. If you reveal more wall the room will appear bigger.
- Less is more. The fewer things there are in a room, the more sense of space. With a property development you can get away with one or two pieces just to suggest how the prospective buyer might use the space.

DOORS

- Doors and doorways are often overlooked, but can have a huge impact on the way we perceive space. Take a tip from grand stately homes if you are completely renovating a period property – align all doorways throughout the ground floor so that light floods in and the eye can see a vast open line from one end of the property to the other. This can be expensive, but if you are replacing walls and doorways or changing the structure of a building anyway it is worth considering.
- In contemporary homes, create doorways that allow the space to be flexible. Concealed doors that slide completely into a cavity wall are ideal. They maximise the sense of space by opening up rooms yet close off the space when privacy is required.
- Modern sand-blasted glass doors can look wonderful but they are expensive, so consider them only for the top-end development.

STORAGE

- Storage helps to keep a space clutter free. Consider concealed storage, tons of cupboards and built-in units that keep surfaces clear and utilities hidden.

Maximising the appeal of your 'buy to let'

Before you embark on any renovation project, you need to know who your market is and how to target their needs accordingly. Furnishing and decorating a 'buy to let' property is no different.

Preparation is paramount. Before you invested in a 'buy to let' property you should have already thought long and hard about the location, size and facilities the property offers, as well as the amenities provided by the local area. You will have determined which sector of the public those particular attributes will appeal to and researched what that market is willing to pay each month in rent, to make sure your investment is financially viable. Finally, and most importantly, you will have checked that there is a demand to rent the property. Now you need to tailor the layout, style and facilities to that market in your renovation.

How to tailor the property to your market

First of all, you need to *know your market*. Think about the standard, type of facilities and furnishings your target tenant will want from a rental property. A corporate client will desire a spacious interior with room for entertaining and a high-spec finish. The student market, on the other hand, will opt for more basic accommodation and a simple, modern decoration scheme.

Check what your market is currently willing to pay to rent your property. Look at similar homes for rent in your area and seek advice from a letting agent. You should have already done this before you purchased the property, but if time has lapsed since you completed contracts, the market may have changed. You need to be up to speed on rental prices so that you can budget for your design scheme accordingly. Planning carefully from the outset will keep you focused on your market (rather than renovating for your own taste) and help you stick to your budget.

Now draft up a schedule of works and a budget. It is essential that you get organised right at the very beginning of the project so that you don't lose momentum along the way. Decide what needs to be done and start to find out how much materials and labour will cost. Be strict with yourself and make changes only in areas that will make your property more lettable. Do not be tempted to take on work that will burden your budget unnecessarily.

Write down everything on a big wall chart, make lists of the work to be done and details for each job including when you have employed contractors and when to expect deliveries. Make sure things happen at the right time. Doing so means that you won't book in the plasterer before the electrician is finished, or the kitchen fitter before the units arrive, for example. Remember, every extra day you add to the schedule puts a strain on your budget.

SEE ALSO

Identifying your target market	p 38
Managing a 'buy to let'	p 91

Designing your scheme

Whatever your market, design and spec, there are some general rules that will stand you in good stead when furnishing a 'buy to let'.

décor

Keep your décor light and bright. For walls, stick to one colour throughout, preferably a neutral colour like off-white or cream. You will find this is easy to maintain and touch up between tenants, it is inoffensive to all and maximises the sense of light and space the property offers. Avoid loud colours and patterned papers, both of which rely on the tenant having the same taste as you.

flooring

To pull your scheme together, think about continuity. Laying the same flooring throughout, for example, can make the rooms flow and look smart. Using different floor colours or material will visually break up the space and make it feel smaller if clashing or strong patterns are used. However, if flooring is used in sympathy with the space it can have the opposite effect.

Think carefully about the type of flooring you use:

- Carpet will stain easily and wear out with heavy foot traffic. If you do choose carpet, avoid light colours for just about all markets, or you will find they need replacing constantly.
- Hardwood and laminate floorings are easier to maintain and keep clean and will currently appeal to a broad section of the market. You can add some rugs to cosy up bedrooms and bring warmth to living rooms in winter.
- Think twice about fitting hardwood flooring or carpet in bathrooms. You will find ceramic tiles or linoleum far more durable and water resistant.

kitchen

Think practical and clean. If installing a new kitchen choose a simple, light-coloured modern design that is easy to maintain and keep clean. Buy cheap and replace it every few years. For worktops, avoid materials that damage, stain or burn easily. Choose a stainless steel sink as it is practical, hard-wearing and easy-to-clean, and do install a splashback for the sink and cooking area to prevent walls getting greasy and grubby.

Make sure all appliances are fully serviced and easy to use. This will help prevent misuse and costly repairs. Leave behind a copy of each instruction manual in a kitchen drawer along with the servicing certificates. Ideally, have a freestanding rather than integrated washing machine and fridge so that if anything goes wrong with either, you can slide it out easily to carry out repairs and a replacement is cheaper.

bathroom

For bathrooms stick to a simple, white suite and provide plenty of splashbacks. It is best to install a good shower if you don't already have one. If the room has a tired but perfectly good bathroom suite for your market, think about scrubbing it up and just replacing the tiles, taps, shower curtain and lavatory suite to give it all a fresh feel.

ventilation and extraction

Make sure all of your rooms have adequate and efficient ventilation and extraction. This will help to prevent the build-up of cooking smells and condensation, and prevent damp and mould, especially in the bathroom.

soft furnishings

Consider wear and tear when investing in soft furnishings. Choose upholstery in dark colours to minimise staining and go for heavy fabrics. Leather may sound like an expensive option but has become cheaper in recent years and you might find a good piece second-hand. It will get better and better with age and wear. Heavy canvas is good, too. Washable loose covers are a good idea for chairs and sofas. You could also protect pieces with a proprietary stain repellent.

Note that as landlord, you are responsible for ensuring the upholstered furniture and soft furnishings you supply, whether new or second-hand, comply with the latest fire-resistance standards. The regulations apply to beds, mattresses and headboards, sofas and armchairs, pillows, scatter cushions and seat pads, and loose and stretch covers for furniture. They require soft furniture to have fire-resistant fillings and the fabric to pass appropriate match- or cigarette-resistance tests. Contact your Local Trading Standards Officer or the Department of Trade and Industry (DTI) for further information.

part- or fully furnished

Don't assume that you have to provide fully furnished accommodation. With the increase in shorter work contracts and thus short lets, many tenants require properties to be furnished. However, 'part-furnished', which means fitted kitchen, bathroom, beds, sofas, dining table, chairs and curtains, is very common and mostly acceptable these days. (Do be aware of your obligations regarding furnishings and fire regulations – see above.) In some areas, unfurnished properties are popular and command a similar rental price. Do your research, get it right for your market and, if in doubt, consult a letting agent.

Think sturdy if you need to buy furniture:

- If buying new tables and chairs go for modern and durable, although old school or church chairs from a junk shop look great in a country-style kitchen when polished up or painted. Students and professionals will want modern basics that take wear and tear – buy copies of designer pieces that you can replace once they go out of fashion. Robust and grand second-hand pieces will look and wear just as well in period properties for family rental.
- You may want to invest in one piece that sets off a room, like a gorgeous mirror. It may be worth spending the extra money, depending on your market.
- If you decide to let a property part-furnished, make sure you provide wardrobes and adequate storage as part of the package.

• If buying new beds, buy cheap and replace them often. You can turn and air a cheap mattress between one or two lets and replace it thereafter. You would be reluctant to throw away an expensive mattress that has become spoilt, but it will really turn off a tenant.

window dressings

Think cheap and cheerful for window dressing. Go for machine-washable curtains or wooden, bamboo or roller blinds that require no maintenance. Look around for fabulous curtain poles that don't cost too much money but give a designer look.

accessories

Always remember that it's a rental property when it comes to accessorising. Don't be tempted to accessorise with expensive items that can be easily broken, and never use sentimental items from your own home. Provide solid, durable pieces that tie in with your scheme and will appear aspirational to your market.

CASE STUDY

Crouch End: Attracting tenants

Katie bought a maisonette above a bookies in Crouch End with her father as a 'buy to let' investment. As a first-time buyer, it was the perfect opportunity for her to climb aboard the property ladder. Katie took on a mortgage and planned to live in the flat when the work was complete and rent out the other rooms, while her dad bought his share of the property as an investment.

PROJECT COSTS – SPLIT 50/50

Cost of property	£185,000
Renovation budget	£20,000
Total investment	£205,000

Anticipated weekly rental income from four rooms at £100 each per week = £400, to be split between Katie and her father

the plan

To keep down costs, Katie decided to decorate and project manage the development herself. She aimed to transform the property into a flat-share for five young professionals. Katie had six months in which to complete the project, absolutely no experience, and had to hold down a full-time job at the same time.

sarah's advice

There was stiff competition. There was a development of 50 luxury apartments being constructed in the area, containing a gym, shops and bars. Many would be bought specifically as 'buy to lets'. The local estate agents I had spoken to confirmed that

Katie's contemporary kitchen was perfect for her buy to let market though the inability to shut this room off from the living space could prove to be a pitfall.

there had also been a boom in privately owned 'buy to let' properties in Crouch End. All of these factors indicated that the market could well be glutted by the time Katie's development would be complete. Always check out the competition and the marketplace before you buy. Katie would have to work much harder at making her flat stand head and shoulders above the professional competition to attract tenants.

I felt that it would be hard for Katie to compete in this market. The young professionals Katie hoped would rent the flat-share would probably have jobs in the city. However, Crouch End had no Underground station and the bus route into central London was slow and complicated. If this is your market, always make sure you invest in an area with good transport links. Secondly, I felt that not only was there a great deal of competition but also that young professionals were more likely to buy a property than to rent and were very unlikely to want to share with so many other people. Katie's more realistic market would be students and low earners, but Crouch End has no colleges or hospitals nearby and the lack of

SEE ALSO

Identifying your target market   p 38

Katie's living area was beautifully finished, although I did wonder if the pale colour scheme and furnishings would withstand the inevitable wear and tear of a buy-to-let.

Katie's flat needed careful designing in order to offer five people privacy as well as space. Katie's initial idea was to locate one of the bedrooms between the living room and the kitchen. However, this would have meant that the bedroom would have been sandwiched between the busiest rooms in the flat while cutting up the available living space. I saw the solution as a change of layout. If the communal rooms were next to each other the living area would be maximised, especially if Katie fitted double doors to open up and close off the living room from the kitchen when required. The fifth bedroom could then be moved to a very private area with a bathroom next door. Katie ended up taking my advice, but also opened up the living room to the kitchen completely to make one open-plan room. This did limit the flexibility of the space, but was definitely an improvement on her first plan.

transport links would deter them, too. The advice is to make sure you know your rental market. Target your location as well as your spec and design accordingly.

Katie's immediate location posed another problem. The noise from the bookies downstairs was coming up into the flat through the floor. Katie was worried it would put off potential tenants and fixing the problem would end up eating into her budget.

how the project progressed

The project got off to a good start. Katie stripped the flat of its lurid colours and blown plasterwork. Yet, with the pressures of a day job and a healthy social life, Katie found it a thankless task and even though she knew it would make for a better finish, the preparation seemed to take forever. It would have been best if Katie had planned the stages of her development while the preparation work was taking place, but she did not plan a schedule of work or a detailed budget to keep her project on track.

Katie's flat needed careful designing so that five people could feel it offered spacious accommodation as well as privacy. I saw one solution as a change of layout. The communal rooms would be best located next to each other to make the flat work – I suggested moving the kitchen to the fifth bedroom so that it could be next to the living room and make the fifth bedroom a very private room with a bathroom next door. Katie did decide to move the kitchen as I had suggested, but was then keen to make the room completely open plan with the living area. With five sharers I would always suggest installing double doors to make the space flexible and private when desired. This gives tenants the option of one or two reception rooms in effect, rather than one big room that feels like a large kitchen with no defined living area.

furnishing the property for tenants

When it came to furnishing the interior, I took Katie to a hip hotel for inspiration. I suggest you do something similar. The top-end cutting-edge design might not be within your budget, but you can borrow some ideas, look at the different materials and see how the professionals put a look together. It is important to tempt tenants at this end of the market with a few luxurious extras, which don't have to cost a fortune. Think about details like colours, mood lighting and light fittings, headboards, curtains and curtain poles, and one or two additional items such as a sculptural vase, sexy mirror or luxurious cushions. These are the sorts of ideas you can emulate quite cheaply in order to create a 'designer' feel …

- Lighting, for example, is key and can go a long way towards creating that luxurious look. Do not always rely on the bare bulb in the middle of a ceiling.
- A mirror can create an opulent focal point and increase the apparent size of the space. Look around local auction houses for a bargain.
- Details make a difference – chrome fittings, door handles and curtain poles look the part, cost less than a tenner and give that hotel feel as Katie discovered.
- If you are lucky enough to have good floorboards, sand and paint or varnish them. They look great and need little maintenance. Katie's light-coloured carpets in the communal hallways and stairs could prove high maintenance, but the white painted floorboards in one of the bedrooms will only improve with wear and age.
- Aim for a light and airy interior. Create a blank canvas for tenants.

SEE ALSO

Choosing the right spec and design for your market   p 102

- A big beautiful plant is an inexpensive way to dress up a room, although you have to rely on your tenant to water it.
- In Katie's flat, the bathrooms would have to accommodate five people all going to work at the same time. Generally, I would advise installing as many bathrooms as possible and fitting them with plain white suites and a shower as well as a standard bath where possible. You would also need to install the correct hot water system so that the hot water doesn't run out for the last person in the bathroom. Make bathrooms as easy to clean as possible with plenty of tiling. Painted walls get grubby quickly and I advise against wallpaper in a bathroom – the steamy atmosphere can make it peel and look untidy. Also install enough storage to organise five people's toiletries. Think practical.
- It sounds obvious, but do measure up before you order. Katie ordered a roll-top bath, which was a decadent option for a rental property and not altogether practical as the plumber couldn't fit it in when it arrived!

the outcome

It took Katie two months longer than she had expected to finish working on her development, which resulted in additional unanticipated mortgage payments. These, together with some overspending meant she went about 50% over her original budget. In the end, Katie and her father decided to sell the property. It was valued by different estate agents at between £275,000 and £325,000.

CHAPTER SUMMARY

1 Always target your design directly towards your intended market.
2 Be aware of your limitations. Know when to call in experts to get a job done.
3 Make sure your development adheres to building regulations every step of the way.
4 Concentrate on maximising light and space in your property.
5 Include elements in your design that will make your property stand out from the competition as the one to buy or rent.
6 Good design need not cost the earth. Think about where best to spend your money and when to cut costs so as to get the look and feel of a property right but within budget.
7 Take inspiration from the design schemes of smart hotels and designer interiors – look at their ideas and the materials used.
8 When furnishing a property for rental, expect wear and tear and be prepared to freshen up your scheme regularly.

SELLING YOUR PROPERTY

Presenting to sell

After months of research, planning, careful budgeting and serious amounts of hard work, you will be itching to know whether all your efforts have paid off financially. In short, you want a sale.

At the time of writing, houses are currently taking longer to sell (up to a month longer) than they did this time last year and sale prices have dropped – some say by as much as 15% at the top end of the market in five months. You will therefore need to work extra hard to clinch a deal. The first step is to present your property for sale.

The good news is that you have a head start over a great deal of the competition. Having just totally refurbished a property you will have taken care of all the practical improvements and the design of the space. You won't have any clutter, pieces of unwanted furniture or too many personal possessions in the space, all of which can be a real turn-off to potential buyers. Furthermore, if you have done your research, the way your property looks will be targeted directly at your particular market, their wants and their needs. In other words, your property should already be highly marketable.

You still, however, need to make an effort! This is the final phase in the development, but it is an important one. Use my three-stage strategy to get things looking great *before* you book in any valuations:

1 Create some kerb appeal.
2 If it doesn't move, clean it!
3 Sell the lifestyle.

Create some kerb appeal

If you have spent months concentrating on the interior of the property, you *must* now give the exterior the facelift it deserves. If you have a front garden, you should have planted any new shrubs and bulbs and done any landscaping a while ago so as to give the garden time to mature. The finishing touches should be to mow the lawn, sweep any pathways and keep them clear of weeds and litter. It may sound obvious, but make sure the skip will be collected in good time and that any dustbins are emptied and tidied away. Next, check any impact the adjoining properties have on your presentation. If your neighbours have left a settee outside for the council to collect or have left a pile of rubbish on view, offer to remove the offending items on your next visit to the local tip. Your aim should be to get viewers from the kerb to your doorway and create a great first impression of a well-maintained and tidy home.

Does the front door need painting or need new door furniture? This is your last chance to remedy things if the entrance looks dull or if the development work has taken its toll. Make sure you scrub the porch and if the entrance still looks lifeless or lacks colour, add a flower box with brightly coloured blooms, a hanging basket or pretty potted shrubs, depending on your market and your property.

Next, get all of the windows cleaned, inside and out. This will make them gleam from the street and illuminate your newly decorated rooms beautifully with natural light.

SEE ALSO

Identifying your target market	p 38
Sell the lifestyle	p 141

If it doesn't move, clean it!

Your next task is to get rid of all of those months' worth of builder's dust and bring out the best in your fixtures and fittings. Set aside at least a whole day for cleaning, unless you choose to call in a professional cleaning company.

Invest in two pairs of industrial-strength gloves, oodles of cleaning products, brand new dusters, sponges, tea towels and any specialist products you may need, like fluid for polishing stainless steel splashbacks. Remember to bring the vacuum, a mop, bucket and dustpan and brush from home. Now photocopy the cleaning checklist on page 140, and take it with you so that you remember everything that needs doing.

SEE ALSO

p 140   Cleaning schedule checklist

Macclesfield: Beating the competition

Bored with the lucrative world of computers, Lisa embarked on her first project as a property developer in Macclesfield, Cheshire. She bought a three-bedroom semi-detached house on a large 1970s estate, which she aimed to transform in just fourteen weeks, while holding down her day job. The property was run down, in need of a new roof, windows, kitchen, bathroom and a garden makeover before redecoration could begin. Decorating is Lisa's passion and she also had big ideas for her little semi, despite a tight budget.

PROJECT COSTS

Cost of property	£110,000
Renovation budget	£15,000
Target resale price	£145,000
Anticipated pre-tax profit	**£20,000**

The plan

With a budget of just £15,000 to transform a three-bedroom house, Lisa couldn't afford to make mistakes. She allowed just £500 to replace and fit a bathroom suite, £2,000 for new windows, patio door and front door and £650 to strip out and replace the leaky flat roof. She did, however, make a huge saving in labour by doing a lot of the jobs herself. Her main saving though came by employing handyman Roger who, fed up of living next door to the tired house, was prepared to do all the heavy work for an amazingly discounted all-in price of just £750 – thousands less than it would normally cost.

Sarah's advice

I hoped that Lisa's sums would add up because she had chosen well and bought a good property in a desirable area. House prices in Macclesfield had risen by an incredible 50% the previous year, faster than anywhere else in the UK. Factories that had once stood empty have been turned into luxury apartments, the town has good

Lisa transformed this lifeless living room into the perfect lounge in her modern family home.

travel links north and south, as well as lush Cheshire countryside five minutes away by car. Lisa had chosen the perfect property and location for a starter family. It was close to the town centre and had amenities on the doorstep. The only danger was that if potential buyers didn't like Lisa's very definite taste, there were plenty of other similar houses to choose from.

Lisa's plans to make the house feel less cramped, introduce an eating area and French windows in the kitchen, which opens on to a newly landscaped garden would all score highly with her target audience and make the property stand out from the competition. Lisa also wanted to add a small conservatory to add more living space to the small house.

In addition, she had to make the small family bathroom feel bigger to achieve top price. Here, Lisa wanted to replace a perfectly good white bath, deck the floor with pebble-effect tiles to give a beach effect and some 'Roman-style' wall tiles. This very busy and defined statement of personal taste could turn off some potential purchasers. As you now know, the key to property developing is to play safe and keep the look neutral and simple. However, keen decorator Lisa had extravagant ideas for every room. Her own house is highly imaginatively designed and her ideas are well put

Lisa's kitchen benefited from an eating area and French windows that opened out onto the garden. This would make her property stand out from the competition.

together, but a developer's property needs to appeal to as many people as possible to sell it quickly, rather than wait for the one person who will fall in love with it.

As with any development, Lisa also needed to keep a tight reign on her budget. Like many people, the bathroom fittings were where she was tempted to get spending, but for this development she shouldn't. If her development was a very high-spec contemporary loft the market would expect top-end fittings and fixtures. In a small three-bedroom family home, they do not. Lisa fell for a corner bath and a sink with a cabinet beneath. I was concerned that both were too big for the room and not really to everyone's taste.

How the project progressed

Just as Lisa spent £1,000 on the bathroom, she stumbled into a problem with the new roof. Through no faulty of her own, Lisa's contractors let her down last minute and the emergency replacement team were charging £860 for labour and a further £450 for scaffolding, which she hadn't budgeted for. Compared with her original estimate of £650, the cost of the roof had suddenly doubled to £1,300. Lisa estimated that she would run £4,000 over budget overall, as other material costs had escalated. She hoped to recoup this in the sale price.

When developing it is a good idea to consult estate agents regularly. With her costs rising, Lisa was smart and called in some advice. The agent advised that while a conservatory may make the property easy to sell it would not actually add value and would have to be within a certain size to comply with permitted development rights.

Good developing is about reducing the risks. The safest thing for Lisa to do at this stage of the project would have been to work out a new budget based on the lowest valuation the estate agents advised. The current ceiling price in the area was £135,000 and, although she was keen to put the house on the market for at least £145,000, Lisa should stick to the £135,000 for her budgeting. Lisa would also have to be careful when she put it on the market as there was a danger that if she overpriced her property it would not sell in a competitive market, with lots of great homes on offer. Every road has a ceiling price – you can punch through the ceiling but only if every single thing in the house is perfect, including the garden.

Lisa completely refurbished the bathroom, but her choice of tiles was personal and may not appeal to all of her viewers.

Lisa was right to start work on the garden early so that it had time to mature and settle before the property went on the market. As well as dealing with the rear garden, she made the most of the front garden – a great relief to see as so many people forget the front garden and the effect it has on prospective purchasers. Unfortunately the garden ended up costing £800 rather than £650 and I wondered at this stage whether Lisa would temper some of her decorating ideas, but she was still keen to impress potential buyers with her distinctive style and pushed on, full steam ahead, to the finish line.

Looking ahead

Lisa also started to look for her next property to develop and was aiming to spend more on the next development. The big problem for amateur developers is getting the timing just right, as it's all about cash flow. The property Lisa chose to view was a semi-derelict 19th-century weaver's cottage. It is worth looking around to see what is available, but don't buy until you are sure you can afford to, however good a deal it may look. Check out the market but don't commit until you have sold the first one. By your second development you should have established a relationship with some suppliers, so this time round you should get better discounts. Second properties are also normally easier as you should have learnt lessons from the first.

The outcome

In just three months Lisa's dilapidated semi had been completely transformed. She had finished on time with the help of Roger and her family. The previously unkempt garden was now an attractive space for children and adults, with a great lawn to play on and a decked terrace for alfresco dining. But it was inside where Lisa had really made her mark.

The once soulless drab reception room had been brought to life by Lisa's designs. The fireplace, although only decorative, provided a focal point. The kitchen was a dramatic transformation, with new French windows giving a sight line through the property to the garden and providing a family dining area. It was a great redesigning of the space and a major improvement to the property.

Upstairs, the whole atmosphere had changed. It was beautifully finished, but Lisa's personal style was everywhere and her rose petal wall on the landing may not have been to everyone's liking. There were more of Lisa's touches in the bathroom, with its pebble-effect floor tiles and busy wall tiles. Despite moving a wall to fit in the new corner bath the room still felt a little cramped. The master bedroom had been decorated in rich green and golds with further attention to detailed presentation, and it felt far more spacious than before. The second bedroom had another theme and had been given a completely different feel with a fresh colour scheme, although the bed, lovely as it was, did dominate the space. The third bedroom was decorated in a different theme again and had very personal staging, which made the room feel smaller than it actually was. It looked great as a design concept but box rooms are generally for children, especially in a three-bedroom house, so for a development the style was a bit too grown-up with personal touches and netting over the bed, which impinged on the visual space. Lisa did not put wardrobes in any of the bedrooms, which could be a problem as storage is paramount for a family. The rule of thumb is, the smaller the room, the more important it is to show how it can be used.

Overall, the finish throughout was excellent but it did come at a cost – £4,000 over budget. Seeing the development come together, Lisa was more confident than ever that she could break through the ceiling price. Everything rested on the estate agents' valuations. The quotes came back at a maximum of £145,000. If Lisa could sell for £145,000 she could recover a £16,000 profit, but Lisa wanted to aim higher and put the house on the market at £150,000. This would give her a £21,000 profit, but only if it sold at that price and fast.

As the viewings started, there were mixed reactions to Lisa's décor. The consensus was that the property was a little overpriced in relation to others the home hunters were viewing in the area. One of the golden rules of property developing is to price your property realistically to sell, in order to get your cash out quickly to move on to the next development. By overpricing the property, Lisa was taking a risk, just as she took the risk decorating in her own personal style. But the finish was so good that if someone came along who liked it, they would love it. As I write, she has indeed had an offer of £150,000.

Lisa decorated her property in her own personal style. Though beautifuly executed, she could have saved money on finishing touches that may not appeal to every viewer.

CLEANING SCHEDULE

☐ Start at the top of the house and clean each room from top to bottom, literally! This way you can ensure that you catch all of the dust as it works its way down the property when you disturb it.

☐ Remove any rubbish or leftover tools from the property, then start by cleaning the highest surfaces, such as the tops of wardrobes and light fittings.

☐ Next, wipe over any pieces of furniture, shelving, door frames and window ledges with a damp cloth to really remove layers of building dust, dirt and grime before dusting.

☐ Clean and polish any pieces of furniture, and vacuum upholstered furniture.

☐ Polish any door handles and other fixtures such as light fittings. Wipe clean any lamp bases and light bulbs. Polish any mirrors or pictures.

☐ Check that there are no signs of any paint on the light switches and sockets, door or window furniture. Gently scrape off any excess paint and wipe them over with a damp cloth.

☐ Use a damp cloth to clean inside any cupboards, cabinets or wardrobes. Viewers always have a desire to open these and you want them to be greeted with a fresh smell and dust-free appearance.

☐ Check all of your lights are fitted with working bulbs. Many professionals choose to view properties after work, in fading light.

☐ Make sure your bathroom suite is immaculate. Scrub and shine up your bath, basin, shower and loo, inside and out. Polish taps and mirrors.

☐ Get the most out of your kitchen. Make sure the oven, hob, fridge and washing machine are all clean and sparkling. Work surfaces should be spotless, taps and door handles should shine. Wipe down cupboards inside and out – your viewers are bound to check out the storage.

☐ Next, dust all of your skirting boards and radiators front and back.

☐ Finally, turn your attention to the floor. Vacuum all of the carpets and any rugs. If you have just had carpet fitted, make sure you suck up any ends left by the fitter. If you have recently polished or painted wooden floors, vacuum them before mopping them with specialist wood cleaner. In bathrooms, vacuum tiled or vinyl floors to get rid of building dust before mopping them with floor cleaner. Don't forget any stairs. If you are not satisfied with the results in any room, do it again, as a clean floor makes a huge difference to the look, smell and feel of a room. If the floor colour is light, it needs to be ultra clean to maximise that reflective surface and bounce light around the room.

Sell the lifestyle

You should know your target market well by now. You will know their expectations, their needs and wants from a property. Your job is to 'tick all the boxes' and provide a few extra aspirational touches at a price they can afford.

It is at this stage of the project that some developers feel it necessary to accessorise each room. Don't be tempted to do this. If you accessorise to your own personal taste, you can needlessly spend large amounts of money, risk putting off viewers with your taste and clutter up the newly decorated space. Keep your look clean and simple. Furthermore, remember with design that less is more. If you have made a good job of your development and it has a beautiful finish, there is no need to overdo it. You should aim to suggest how the viewer could live in the property, nothing more.

If, however, you have awkward spaces, feel that the rooms need defining or are missing a certain something, look at the following quick, simple tips.

Furniture

It is never a good idea to buy a lot of furniture to decorate a property you are about to sell. You may not be able to reuse the pieces in your next development and will have to pay to put the furniture in storage. You can stage a property for sale with furniture from your own home, pieces borrowed from friends and family or hired specifically for the purpose.

Make sure that what you do put into a room suggests how that space can best be used. For example, if you have room for an eating area in a kitchen, add a table and chairs to illustrate the point. If you have a box room, put in a single bed to show that it is big enough to do so. Similarly, if you have a small bedroom put a bed in to suggest to the buyer how they could use the room. You can pick up second-hand bases and mattresses very cheaply. Once swathed in crisp white linen they will look as impressive and inviting as brand new.

However, don't let furniture dominate your rooms. Whatever you do, don't be tempted to fill your rooms with too much, or add pieces that are too large or imposing for the space. You will make the rooms look smaller and moving around the space feel awkward. Arrange furniture to maximise all of the available space. If you do hire any items of furniture, make sure that the colours and styles you choose complement your décor.

Create a focal point

Use mirrors strategically in the presentation of your property. Placing a mirror in a narrow room will create a sense of depth. In a dark room, it will bounce and reflect light; in a small room, it will increase the sense of space.

If you are short of a great view, cheat by adding a wonderful picture or painting from your home or a second-hand shop to create a focal point.

The finishing touches

Leave bedrooms clean, calm and simple. Dress beds with fresh, crisp linen, preferably white. Keep the kitchen free of clutter – don't be tempted to add china, pots and pans. A bowl of fruit or a plant will add life and colour; a lovely bottle of olive oil will add

TIP

Forget trying to beat estate agents to viewings in order to grind fresh coffee, bake vanilla pods and fresh bread! The old clichés may work but they are also highly impractical! Your property should smell clean after all your scrubbing – all you should need do now is make sure you open all of the windows to let in some fresh air.

elegance and break up an empty work surface and an inexpensive, but designer-looking, kettle on a hob can look both stylish and homely.

Suggest the bathroom is a place in which to relax and experience a little luxury by buying some inexpensive, fluffy white towels to place over towel rails if the space looks too clinical.

The living room should feel inviting. Some spaces look best left bare, others need a helping hand. If you have a less-than-desirable view from a window, invest in a simple blind, or hang a bolt of fabric from a pole to detract attention from outside. Beware of spending money on having curtains made as you might never use them again, and you want to be careful not to block out too much light. Leave furniture simple. If the space looks cold, bring some warm colour co-ordinated cushions from your own home or buy some inexpensive ones from a homeware store. You could also consider a green leafy, flowering plant or an orchid to add life to your scheme, then take them home or give them away as gifts when you sell the property, or leave them as a housewarming present for the purchaser. Another way to add warmth is with clever lighting. If you have a separate dining room, put in a table and chairs in scale with the room.

Getting a valuation and choosing an estate agent

Once your property looks irresistible, it is time to get a valuation. Start by choosing your estate agents carefully.

You should look for three reputable agents based in your area to come and give you a valuation of the property. If you bought the property from an estate agent and were happy with their services, then they are a good place to start. To find two others, look at the companies most actively marketing homes for sale in your area. Does the estate agent have regular advertisements in the local press, a comprehensive and easy-to-use website with links to property portals and lots of 'sold' or 'for sale' boards dotted around your neighbouring streets? These are all good signs.

To save on time, book in staggered appointments for all your agents to view the property on the same day. Now you have finished the development, you don't want to keep flitting back and forth and you'll want to get the property on the market as soon as possible.

However, *before* you make those appointments, do your research:
- Look at the local property press, estate agents' websites and property details through the eyes of a buyer.
- Check the sale prices being commanded by properties similar to your own. Get a feel for the market – it may have changed since you bought the property.
- See how many properties similar to yours are currently for sale. This is important. If there is a glut of properties similar to your own on the market you will need to be even more realistic about your asking price, unless you are offering something extra. Remember the property market works on the laws of supply and demand. The greater the demand for your property, the higher the asking price you can expect to achieve.

Be realistic about your asking price and be wary of an agent who gives you an inflated estimate. If you have done your research you should be able to spot this.

TIP

When you ring to book a valuation, ask the agent to bring to the appointment details of properties they have recently sold that are similar to yours. The prices that these homes actually sold for will give you a better indication of the market than the asking prices the owners hoped to achieve.

SARAH SUGGESTS ... 'A common mistake made by home owners when selling is to be flattered by the highest valuation they receive and choose that agent to sell the property. The reality is that a house is worth only what a purchaser will pay for it and remember that an estate agent is not a buyer.'

Employing an estate agent

Now you need to decide which estate agent to market your property with. Do you choose one or several agents to try and sell it? See the table opposite for a quick run-down of the pros and cons of sole or multiple agents.

Before you make your decision about which agent to appoint, use these three tips for finding the right agent:

1   **Did you like the estate agent?** Were they friendly, personable and professional? Not only will you need to work closely with your agent, but you want on board someone who will be polite, approachable and well informed to meet viewers, show them around the property and negotiate on your behalf.

2   **Have you checked the company terms and conditions?** Always read the small print to ensure you won't be tied into an agreement that doesn't suit you, such as having to keep the property on their books for a prolonged length of time.

3   **Do you know what you are getting for your money?** It may sound obvious, but check exactly where and how your property will be marketed. Ask how many viewings the agent expects to line up over the first few weeks.

Selling privately

This is another possible option, but the pitfalls outweigh the benefits and I would rarely recommend you plunge for a private sale. Although the obvious advantage is that there is no need to pay agents' fees, you will have to market the property yourself. This means you need to be incredibly organised and always available to conduct viewings. You will need to negotiate a sale price yourself, whereas an agent can act as a mediator on your behalf and justify an asking price. You will undoubtedly have less resources, and certainly less experience, than the agent to carry out all of these important tasks effectively and remember, there is a lot of money at stake if you get any of these things wrong.

TIP
If you sign a sole agency agreement with more than one estate agent, you may find you are legally obliged to pay fees twice.

SARAH SUGGESTS ... 'Personally, I would always sell a property I have spent time, effort and money developing through an agent. Don't be fooled into thinking you will save yourself money on commission fees when there are large sums of cash at stake. There is too much at risk if you can't carry out any of the tasks involved in selling as professionally as an agent. In any case the chances are pretty high that with all of their marketing skills and resources an agent will get more for your property than you would, which will negate any fee you have to pay them.'

OPTING FOR SOLE, JOINT OR MULTIPLE AGENT

AGENT TYPE	PROS	CONS
Sole agent You instruct only one estate agent to market and sell your property.	An estate agent will offer you favoured rates of commission if you go solely through them (around 2%). When the property goes under offer, you are more easily able to control it being taken off the market and viewings to cease.	You will need to sign a contract to say that the property is being marketed and handled by only one company. If you are not happy with the service or decide you want to enlist the services of more estate agents, you sometimes need to wait a period of time before you are able to do so.
Joint sole agents Two estate agents market the property for sale and split the fee between them on an agreed basis when one sells it – usually about 75% to the successful estate agent and 25% to the unsuccessful agent.	Doubles your chances of finding a buyer.	An estate agent is less likely to put as much effort into selling your property if there is a chance another agent may find a buyer just as they come up with one. The successful agent has to give a percentage of their commission to the other agent who has done absolutely nothing in terms of their sale – understandably this sits bitterly with many agents.
Multiple agents You employ two or more estate agents to market and sell your property.	The increased coverage and marketing will get your property seen by a wider market. You pay a commission only to the agent who sells the property.	The rate of commission due to the estate agent is higher – around 3.5%. If you decide to employ multiple agents, but have received different valuations, you will need to negotiate the asking price you would like and put the property up for sale with all of the agents at the same level. It won't look good if home hunters view your property at one price and see it advertised for another elsewhere. Putting your property up for sale with several agents can send signals to possible home hunters that it has been on the market for so long that either there is a problem with it or it is overpriced. Neither is appealing to a prospective purchaser.

Working with your estate agent

Once you have chosen your agent, you will need to work at building a good rapport with them.

If they like and respect you, they will do more to help sell your property. And, if you are planning on developing property in the local area in the future, then building up a good relationship with an agent you trust is paramount. Whatever your situation you want to get the most out of the agent–vendor relationship:

1 **Commission**. In theory, an estate agent's commission fee is negotiable. However, don't haggle over 0.5 or 1%. It will make little difference to your gross profit and could scupper your relationship. The last thing you want is for the agent to put less effort into selling the property for less commission.

2 **Negotiate a contract**. Negotiate to put your property on with an agent for the minimum contract time – usually four weeks. During this initial period the estate agent will have an influx of viewers lined up from their existing database of home hunters. After this initial glut of viewings, you will be relying on new customers signing up with the agent. If you are pleased with the service the estate agent has offered towards the end of the contract time and with the number of viewings taking place, then extend the contract.

3 **Marketing details**. When you have discussed the sale price and the commission fee, the estate agent will compile written details and take photographs of the property for marketing. Make sure you are happy with the photographs they plan to use. Check that they were taken in sunlight and are in colour. A bad picture could put off home hunters from booking a viewing. Estate agents are legally obliged to give correct and accurate details of the property. Mistakes do happen, however, so do check the details yourself. Ensure the right descriptions of the property and measurements of the rooms appear. Make sure that the best features are mentioned, as well as sought-after extras like the garden, good storage and parking, and the proximity of the property to the nearest travel links and amenities.

4 **Viewings**. Let the agent conduct the viewings. This will allow the home hunter to feel comfortable and be objective. It will also mean they can meet the agent who will be negotiating on your behalf if they decide to put in an offer.

5 **Communication**. Organise a specific occasion each week when you and your agent will speak about the viewings that have taken place. This will allow the agent sufficient time to gather any information ready for your call and save you making umpteen calls while your agent is out of the office. During these conversations, ask for any feedback from viewings and the number of parties that they have shown around the property. Avoid trying to justify any negative criticism to the agent, jot down the feedback quietly and think about it. If you find certain comments crop up time and time again, think about how you could redress the problem to make the property more desirable to viewers, or drop the price accordingly. Respond to any queries the agent has quickly and professionally.

6 **Building work and guarantees**. Keep information about any work you have had carried out on the property in a box file. This should include any certificates for works,

building regulation and planning permission certificates. Send a full copy of these not only to your estate agent in case of enquiries but also to your solicitor in preparation for a sale.

Also keep handy the guarantees for any appliances or white goods, any service history you have for a boiler and the manual for how to work the central heating system. These will help the estate agent and the buyer.

How to find a solicitor

If you don't already have a solicitor whom you rely on, you will need to find one and fast.

A good solicitor is crucial. Do not necessarily go for one who happens to be nearby or is recommended by your estate agent. Instead, ask friends or relatives whether they have recently used a solicitor for conveyancing (the legal business of transferring property from one owner to another) with whom they were happy. Remember, we are now in the 21st century and with modern technology your solicitor could be several hours' drive away without it making any difference to your working relationship. The most important thing is that they are good, reliable and efficient as they will be representing your interests. Remember to ask the solicitor for a breakdown of their conveyancing fees before you give them the go ahead to do any work on your behalf.

ANOTHER EXPERT'S WORDS …

One solicitor advises: 'Find out whether your solicitor provides a "no move, no fee" service – it could save you a lot of money.'

TIP
A solicitor is a general legal practitioner who can deal with a variety of legal issues, including house buying and selling; a licensed conveyancer specialises in property transactions.

RESPONSIBILITIES OF THE BUYER'S AND SELLER'S SOLICITORS

- Acting on their client's behalf in all matters.
- Carrying out local authority and other searches on the property. This is done by the buyer's solicitor and includes checking that the seller does in fact own the property and that a motorway is not just about to be built in the field next door!
- Drawing up the contract. This is done by the seller's solicitor and includes supplying pre-contract information such as any fixtures and fittings that are to be included in the sale price and answering a standard set of enquiries on the property being sold.
- Organising the exchange of contracts.
- Organising the transfer of monies, including a deposit, calling down the buyer's mortgage loan and paying off the seller's mortgage.
- Organising the transfer of title deeds, ultimately to the buyer or their lender.

What to do when you receive an offer

When someone decides your property could be their home, they will put in an offer through your estate agent.

You need to think carefully before accepting an offer. If you receive an offer less than the full asking price it could be because the buyer does not feel that the property is worth that amount. Alternatively, they may be trying to get a good deal, or perhaps are unable to borrow the full amount from their mortgage lender. It is important to gauge your buyer's circumstances. You need to know whether they have a home to sell, whether they have an agreement in principle to a mortgage or how they intend to pay for your property. All of these factors will allow you to weigh up the pros and cons of the offer. If they are part of a chain of buyers and sellers relying on each other and one sale falls through, everyone else could lose out. Whatever their situation, don't rush into accepting the first offer you receive if it is lower than your realistic expectations. Consult with your estate agent. They will be working to sell your property as quickly as possible and help you achieve the best price possible, which in turn bolsters their commission fee.

If the offer you receive is a reasonable one, the first decision you will need to make is whether to keep the property on the market or to mark it as 'sold subject to contract'. Generally, the offer will be based on you taking the property off the market, but if you do want to carry out more viewings and continue advertising the property to invite more offers, then you should tell the buyer. In England and Wales you can technically accept other offers until the moment you exchange contracts. However, the buying and selling of property in Scotland is different from the rest of the UK. If this is something you are not aware of take specialist legal advice.

Ask your solicitor to get confirmation that the purchaser's solicitors have been instructed, and to draw up a draft contract. Your purchaser will generally want to carry out local authority and other searches. Encourage their solicitor through your estate agent and your solicitor to get these requested as they do take time. The government target is for local authorities to turn around a search within ten days, but realistically it varies between different local authorities from one or two days to several weeks.

Valuation and survey

The buyer will almost certainly need to have the condition and value of your property checked. Their mortgage lender will organise a valuation to ensure their investment is safe and the buyer will probably arrange for a survey to be carried out.

If the valuation or survey show up any problems, your estate agent will advise you on the appropriate course of action to take. This could involve:

- Lowering your price to continue with the sale.
- Taking the property off the market while you fix the problem and putting it back on the market at a later date.
- Arranging for specialist reports to assess the seriousness of any fault found.

TIP
Abandoning a purchaser in the hope of a quick sale with another buyer is a false economy. The same flaws are likely to show up on their survey, too.

SEE ALSO

The survey	p 26
Buying property in Scotland	p 31

Clinching the deal

Congratulations! After all your hard work it is time for contracts to be exchanged between both parties' solicitors. Once you have exchanged contracts, you and your buyer are legally committed to one another and the buyer's deposit (normally about 10%) will be paid into your solicitor's account to be held for you until completion. Completion – when the transfer of ownership of the property passes from the seller to the buyer – often takes place about four weeks after exchange of contracts, although it depends on both parties' preferences. The time scale can be longer or it is possible to exchange and complete on the same day.

On completion you will receive from the buyer, via your solicitor, the outstanding balance for the sale of your property, less any fees and your mortgage repayment.

Now is the time for you to take a rest, celebrate, or start looking for your next property to develop!

Selling property in Scotland

Scotland has a different system from England and Wales for buying and selling property.

In Scotland, solicitors not estate agents sell the majority of houses. If you ask your solicitor to sell your house, you should expect him or her to provide a full estate agency service. As well as conveyancing, this will include registering your property in the local solicitor's property centre. The solicitor is likely to charge a percentage fee to cover both the selling and the conveyancing and it is sensible to get an estimate for this before going ahead.

You can sell your property through an estate agent but they will normally pass to your solicitor any formal offers that are made.

The next step is to advertise the property for sale – something your solicitor or estate agent can organise for you. In Scotland it is usual to state an asking price and invite offers over this amount. The asking price you put in your advertisement should normally be the minimum figure that you would consider accepting. Your solicitor will advise you on both the price you should ask and the price you should expect to achieve.

When someone is interested in your property, their solicitor will contact your solicitor or estate agent to tell them they have an interested party.

If several people are interested in your house it is usual to fix a closing date for offers – a date and time when you will consider all offers that have been lodged. At this point you will have to decide which offer to accept. You are not obliged to accept the highest offer or any of the offers if you do not wish to do so.

Once you decide to accept an offer your solicitor will liaise with the buyer's solicitor to ensure all points of the sale are agreed. These agreed points are then confirmed in writing and this exchange of letters is referred to as the 'missives'. This process takes only a day or two and it is worth noting that the conclusion of

SEE ALSO

p 31   Buying property in
       Scotland

SEE ALSO

Resources   p 154

missives constitutes a binding contract from which neither side can withdraw. The short time between offers being made and becoming binding and the absence of gazumping are the advantages of the Scottish system.

When the missives have been concluded your solicitor will finalise the conveyancing. He or she will arrange for the title deeds of the property to be sent to the buyer's solicitor, inform your bank or building society that missives have been concluded and obtain a redemption statement to show the amount of your loan to be repaid on completion of the sale.

For more information on selling a property in Scotland you can investigate the relevant websites listed in the resource list on page 155.

Selling property in Ireland

Selling property in Ireland is again slightly different to selling in England and Wales. The large majority of property in Ireland is sold by private treaty, and it is advisable to use a real estate agent to conduct the sale for you. It is common in Ireland for agents to also be auctioneers and it is recommended that you chose an agent who is a member of the Irish Auctioneers & Valuers Institute.

Your agent can place a suggested price level on the property on your behalf, though this price is not binding on the seller. Once your property has grabbed the attention of potential buyers offers will be invited. You would hope to have interest from various parties and to have bid and counter offer at this point. If there is very strong interest in the property, the agent may suggest a closed or private tender. This is essentially a closed competition of final bids from each buyer, with the highest bid winning.

Once you have accepted an offer, it is normal to look for a deposit, usually this is 5% with private treaty sale. Your agent should also ensure that your buyer has funds or an approved loan in place at this point. It is normal to cease to actively market the property at this stage, however the sale is not secured until formal contract documentation has been issued, signed and exchanged by both you and the buyer. Up until this point you may entertain all offers even though you have already accepted an offer. Gazumping does occur.

It is also not uncommon for homes in Ireland to be sold by auction, but it is recommended that you employ an agent who are licensed auctioneers if you choose to sell this way. Check agents in your area and look at the prices they have achieved for homes like yours. There are many good reasons for selling by auction, chiefly that it is quick and you have a defined period in which the sale will, hopefully, take place.

You should expect regular feedback from the agent about how much interest there is in your property and approximately what price to expect from the auction. Based on this, you and the agent will be able to set your confidential reserve price just before the auction. During the auction, the auctioneers will try to get your price up as far as they can. Once the reserve price has been met, the auctioneer will let the audience know and announce that the property is now 'on the market'. The onus is then on all potential buyers to bid competitively for your property. If the worst occurs and your

SEE ALSO

Buying property   p 33
in Ireland

Resources   p 154

house does not meet the reserve price and does not sell your agent can advise you on continuing negotiations with those bidders there were interested in the property. In this way there is every chance that you can still make a sale,

Once all bids are in and the property has sold, the auctioneer and buyer sign the contract the agent has prepared on your behalf and the sale is unconditional. The purchaser pays a 10% deposit on the auction day and settlement of the balance is normally in about 30 days time.

CHAPTER SUMMARY

1 Create some kerb appeal, make sure the property is spotlessly clean and sell the lifestyle by adding a few finishing touches before you put your property on the market.
2 When you present a property for sale, use accessories only to suggest how the viewer could live there.
3 Do your research, and target your property at a specific market.
4 Be realistic about your asking price.
5 Work at getting the most out of the agent–vendor relationship.
6 The best way to find a good solicitor is through a recommendation.
7 When an offer is made on your property, weigh up the pros and cons before you accept.

RESOURCES
AND
INDEX

Resources

Association of Residential
Letting Agents (ARLA)
www.arla.co.uk
0845 345 5752

Centre for Economics
Business Research
www.cebr.com
020 7324 2850

Council of Mortgage Lenders
www.cml.org.uk
020 7437 0075

Department of Trade and Industry
(DTI) – *A Guide to the Furniture and
Furnishings (Fire) (Safety) Regulations*
www.dti.gov.uk
020 7215 5000

DfES School and College Peformance
Tables
www.dfes.gov.uk/perfomancetables
0845 933 3111

Environment Agency
www.environment-agency.gov.uk
0845 93 33 111

Her Majesty's Land Registry
www.landreg.gov.uk
020 7917 8888

Homecheck: Property advice website
www.homecheck.co.uk

Homesale network property website
www.home-sale.co.uk

Hometrack: Prices and market trends
www.hometrack.co.uk

Independent Financial Advisors
Promotion
www.ifap.org.uk
0800 085 3250

Inland Revenue
www.inlandrevenue.gov.uk
0845 605 5999

Irish Law Society
www.lawsociety.ie
00 353 1671 0711

Irish Property News
Property information service
www.irishpropertynews.com
00 353 91 565622

Leasehold valuation tribunals: The
Leasehold Advisory Service
www.lease-advice.org.uk
0845 345 1993

Micropal: Standard & Poors
Investment Information
www.funds-sp.com

National Approved Letting Scheme
www.nalscheme.co.uk
01242 581 712

National Association of Estate Agents
(NAEA)
www.naea.co.uk
01926 496 800

National House Building Council
www.nhbc.co.uk
01494 735 363

National Land Information Services
www.nlis.org.uk
01279 451 625

National Rail Enquiries
08457 484950

Office for Standards in Education
(Ofsted)
www.ofsted.gov.uk
020 7421 6800

Office of the Deputy Prime Minister
(ODPM)
www.housing.odpm.gov.uk
020 7944 4400

Online estate agents
www.findaproperty.com

Rightmove: property advice website
www.rightmove.co.uk

Royal Institute of Chartered Surveyors
(RICS)
www.rics.org.uk
0870 333 1600

Scottish Law Information
www.scottishlaw.org.uk

Scottish Law Society
www.lawscot.org.uk
0131 226 7411

The Historic Buildings
Bureau for Scotland
www.historic-scotland.gov.uk
0131 668 8668

The Law Society
www.lawsociety.org.uk
020 7242 1222

The Society of Financial Advisors
www.sofa.org
020 8989 8464

Trading Standards Office
www.tradingstandards.gov.uk

Up My Street
www.upmystreet.com

Index

CONCLUSION

To all of you who have just read this book I trust you have found it helpful.

Since the creation of the television series *Property Ladder* a couple of years ago, I have had the extraordinary experience of being afforded the luxury of a glimpse into the media world, which is so different to that of building, which I have been used to for so long. It has confirmed one thing in my mind though, which is that if property is in your blood you can't get it out … Wherever in the country we end up filming on location the estate agents' boards dotted about the area are extra little highlights in the day for me!

So, if you have a genuine interest in buildings and why and how we live in them, then perhaps property development is the career for you. If so, I wish you the very best of luck – if not, have the courage to hold your head up high when you admit you don't know where your nearest DIY centre is. After all, there is no sin in your house simply being your home.

Good luck to you all!

Sarah Beeny

I would like to dedicate this book to my mother who would have encouraged me and my father and stepmother who do.

Author's acknowledgements

A special thanks to all the developers we have featured from *Property Ladder*, and to Polly Powell, Samantha Scott-Jeffries, Charlie Bunce, Jude Coker, Kate Morrow, Karen Robinson, Jonny Pollard, Claire Hobday, Jessica Stoddart, Lucie Donahue, Vanessa Cole, Graham Sherrington, Rachel Willis, Lisa Ruff, Laura Hill, Amy Clark, Katie Cowan, John Silver, Ben Frow, Graham Swift, Richard Beeny, Diccon Beeny, John Naylor, Jan Boothroyd at NLIS, Melfyn Williams at NAEA, David Galman at Galliard Homes, Mark Lane at Wriglesworth PR, Stephen Ludlow at Ludlow Thompson, Elliot Nathan at Bradford & Bingley, Andrew Burrell at Experian Business Research, Mike Goddard at Belvoir Lettings, Peter Rollings at Foxtons, Jessica Southgate at CEBR, James Duffell at One Account, Ray Boulger, John Charcoal, Louis Armstrong and Kate Bourne at RICS and Catherine O'Flaherty.

Essential Works' acknowledgements

Editorial: Jo Lethaby and Barbara Dixon
Additional Research: Ruth Carpenter
Design and Illustration: Barbara Saulini
Special Photography: James Bareham
Stylist: Gemma Shanley
Make-up: Panilla Marott and Martyn Fletcher
Screen Grabs: Nats and Exposure
Graph page 10: An Illustrated Guide to
the British Economy, Bill Jamieson, Duckworth 1998